THE AMERICA'S CUP AND ME

By Edward du Moulin

Recollections of 63 years and 7 Campaigns

Herreshoff Marine Museum Press Bristol, Rhode Island 2001

DEDICATIONS

To my late mother Adele, for whom the *Lady Del*s are named, and Cousin Sam Lauterbach, who introduced me to sailing at an early age.

To my late wife Eleanor, for her 58 years of not-just-sailing encouragement, and for playing a vital role in our America's Cup adventures. I will direct the reader to the following tribute written for Eleanor by Halsey Herreshoff. She is greatly missed.

To my son Richard, with whom I have shared my love of sailing since he was three years old, and to his wonderful wife Ann. Together they have added four more sailors to the family: Lora Ann (sailing for Boston College), Edward, Matthew, and Mark. They will carry on the family tradition, representing the fourth generation on the water – over 100 years.

To my late daughter Cathy who put up such a brave fight, and her husband Jerome Morea, a son to Eleanor and to me. They gave us three wonderful grandchildren, Carrie Adele, Douglas (at the Naval Academy), both are sailors, and Christopher, who also sails but is more heavily into lacrosse at Cornell.

And finally, to all of the varied and wonderful sailing companions with whom I have shared my racing, America's Cup, and now cruising years. Many appear in this book.

ISBN 0-9710678-1-3

Library of Congress Control Number:
2001092106

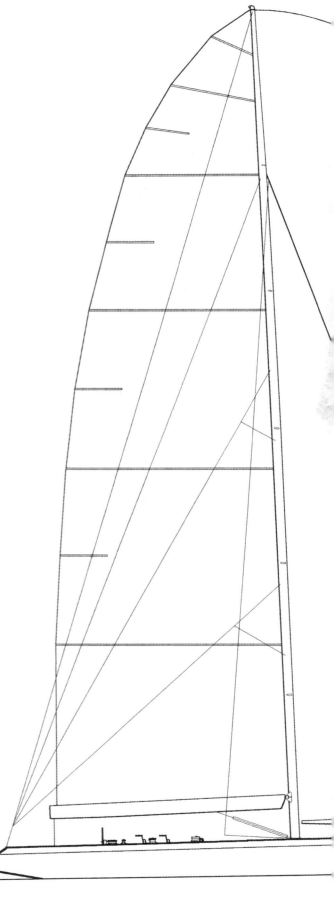

CONTENTS

FOREWORD

In September 2000, Ed du Moulin was inducted into the America's Cup Hall of Fame at the Herreshoff Marine Museum in Bristol, Rhode Island. He thus joined the ranks of John Cox Stevens, George Schuyler, C. Oliver Iselin, Frank Murdock, and E.D. Morgan, all of whom had been, as had Ed, distinguished managers of America's Cup syndicates.

Ed du Moulin epitomizes what is best in America's Cup participants. As leader, manager, organizer, mentor, and confidant, Ed was both the stable center of and the glue for each campaign he managed or advised. His influence upon Dennis Conner and all of us will sustain for the rest of our lives.

The grandeur of the America's Cup transcends the dramatic races that have thrilled generations of young and old for 150 years. Cup campaigns involve vision, courage, financial muscle, research, design, construction, crew selection, training, yacht and sail development. Few campaigns in any sport involve the lengthy intensity of modern America's Cup competition. Typically three years in duration, campaigns that succeed are consuming, never predictable, and totally intriguing.

The high caliber of technical advancement represented by Cup yachts and gear is exceeded only by the interplay and complexity of the human endeavors that are involved. Teamwork of this level and quantity seems to bring out the best – and the worst – in people. Without a steady hand on the wheel of the organization, the most talented crew and the best financed campaign is ill-fated.

The brilliant performances achieved in many of the campaigns of the last quarter of the 20th century depended in large part upon the genius of Ed du Moulin as either manager or respected advisor. This book is a captivating read about some of the challenges Ed faced, and the solutions he helped forge.

Those of us privileged to sail in Ed's syndicates hold him and his late wife

Eleanor in the highest regard. To the syndicate heads, Edward du Moulin was the attentive, reliable organization man and financial manager. To the skipper he was a benchmark of strength, stability, and resourcefulness. To the contributors, he was the fully ethical leader of impeccable credibility who only called when necessary, and who made sure that every commitment was met. To the young crew members he was always cheerful, steadily optimistic, fair and relentless at solving problems. All of us learned method and technique from Ed, lessons that have stayed with us. Ed epitomizes the definition of a gentleman as one who never, ever gets frazzled.

We all know that true history is hard to define – or discover. Many books about events are superficial, lacking in perception, or worse, may present personal prejudice. A good history must be objective, but it is only truly enlightening if it goes deep into the events and the human nuances that guided them. That is why Ed du Moulin's reflections on the America's Cup are so valuable. Ed was there, he touched every element and, most importantly, he is big enough to state all that is relevant without prejudice.

Ed continues today as a trusted advisor to Dennis Conner and others at the top of the sport of sailing. He has been highly instrumental in the formation of the permanent America's Cup Hall of Fame. When you send Ed a fax or an e-mail, count on an answer about as soon as you walk across the room; his decisiveness is as impressive as his wisdom is valuable.

We at the Herreshoff Marine Museum are privileged to publish this volume. It is the best sort of perspective one could have of competing for the ultimate prize in sailing. Ed du Moulin provides a significant addition to the literature defining America's Cup events.

Halsey C. Herreshoff
President, America's Cup Hall of Fame

COHORTS

Ed du Moulin's friends, family and associates know him to be a competitor, a teacher, a sailing advocate, a supporter of sailing competition at all levels, and a devoted family man. In each of these areas, Ed has been a leader and has enjoyed great success. But most of all, Ed likes to be known as a sailor.

My association with Ed and his family has revolved around America's Cup competition, starting with the *Enterprise* campaign of 1977. I was the chairman of the syndicate, and Ed was our general manager. Our campaign turned out to be a real test of character. It was saved from being a disaster by what we learned about organizing a winning team, an invaluable experience.

Ed and I developed a mutual respect that resulted from having to make many tough decisions together. There were also many good times shared as well during this campaign. We both loved sailing and more than ever wanted to defend the America's Cup. This led to joining forces with Dennis Conner for the 1980 campaign.

We agreed that Dennis would be the skipper and in charge of sailing operations. Ed and I took the responsibility for the support side, for administration, and for fund raising. It was a competitive combination, and we went on to successfully defend the Cup with *Freedom* in the 1980 campaign.

I attribute much of our success to Ed. He brought honesty, integrity, a strong sense of fairness and diplomacy, along with consummate business skills to the team – and Ed is always a team player. In contrast with the America's Cup-sized egos that surround him, Ed is a modest man. This allows him to use persuasion when others would use force. Ed personifies the best in a side of America's Cup competition that is behind the scenes. The general public sees only the skipper, the crew, and the racing yacht. That is just the tip of the iceberg. A winning crew requires a competitive support team, and Ed was always at the core of the effort.

It pleased me greatly that in the millennium year 2000, Ed was inducted into the America's Cup Hall of Fame. While this honored Ed's leadership role in America's Cup competition, it also recognized Ed du Moulin, the sailor.

George Frederick Jewett, Jr.

Ed du Moulin's principle contribution to the America's Cup has been the introduction of professional management to entry-level syndicates. In this regard, he became my mentor during his management of the 1977, 1980, and 1983 America's Cup events. Many times thereafter did I seek him out for advice during my management of the 1987 and 1988 Stars & Stripes syndicate efforts, as well as during my General Manager's role in the overall 1992 America's Cup event.

A veteran Wall Street investment banker, Ed had foreseen the steep rise in America's Cup competition, a development which would necessitate more crew, boats, auxillary equipment, supporters, housing needs, and of course, the commensurate increase in financing. Thus, Ed quietly and efficiently brought modern business methods to America's Cup organization, including budgets, time-lines, assignments of individual responsibilities, punctuality, management meetings, and appropriate and timely reporting of all.

Ed has always been known as fair, firm, and diplomatic. It would be considered oxymoronic for most of us to attempt to meld all of those characterists into our personalities. This is simply a natural state for Ed.

Lastly, I would like to mention a side of Ed, little known to the outside world: he often sought advice from his late wife Eleanor as to positioning and dealing with difficult and sensitive situations involving personalities. I am sure

Eleanor's influence bolstered Ed's natural proclivities toward the "fair, firm, and diplomatic."

Malin Burnham

The competition for the America's Cup presents us with more than a boat show; it offers a revealing "people" show as well. Competitors and organizers ride an emotional roller coaster during these long campaigns that can test everyone's limits. Through several America's Cups I have had the opportunity to watch Ed du Moulin handle both the highs and the lows of America's Cup campaigning, and he does it with amazing balance. Ed knows how to level the peaks with reality, and use that same agent to help fill in the valleys. In 1977 when his boat was eliminated, he declared that "the Cup is not a funeral. It is a sailboat race. We will do better next time."

In 1983 Ed du Moulin was associated with the *Liberty* campaign. His boat defeated Tom Blackaller's *Defender* 12 to 8 in a hard set of defense trials. It was a sad day for those of us on *Defender*'s crew when she was eliminated. *Liberty*'s skipper, Dennis Conner, and his crew left the docks to avoid the elimination ceremony. But Ed du Moulin and Fritz Jewett had the courage and good sportsmanship

to come to the *Defender* compound and thank our crew for pushing their crew so hard. It was a gesture of extraordinary class.

As a cadet at the Maritime College, I remember frequently racing against Ed du Moulin's red-hulled *Blaze* on Long Island Sound. Ed and his son Richard were always at the front of fleet, sailing hard and smart.

Ed is a fierce competitor, as well as being naturally considerate. He always remembers your name. Ed is good at the boat show, as the record reflects, and good at the people show, too.

Gary Jobson

Sailing is a team sport requiring substantial amounts of organization, logistics, communication, and personnel management skills. Any racing yacht's success, including the performance of the crew, evolves directly from the skills and management style of the owner or skipper.

Many examples of yachting success through resource management are mentioned in this book. All the players in the sport know that there are good, bad, and ugly programs. Some competitors only show up for one campaign. Others become bastions of the sport, managing successful campaigns for many seasons.

Ed du Moulin is a wonderful example of the latter type, and of the success and longevity possible in our sport. In my opinion, his style encompasses a unique subtlety that sets him apart. Over the years, he has become a quiet giant in the sailing world.

Ed has had enormous impact on the lives of those fortunate enough to have worked with him on his own boats and during his many America's Cup campaigns. And for those lucky enough to have sailed with him on his own boats – *Sprinkhaan*, *Blaze*, and four *Lady Del*s – the experience has been both lasting and inspiring.

Never one to seek the spotlight, Ed has worked tirelessly behind the scenes. He manages by listening, asking opinions, and then synthesizing a way to integrate various ideas into a better whole. When money has been tight, and when equipment has been tired, I have seen Ed work with positive dedication to make the absolute best of the moment.

I have learned from his example that positive programs absolutely do have positive effects. Involvement with any of Ed's projects has changed many lives for the better, mine included. Whatever success I have had with grand prix sailing – and in some measure with all aspects of my life – stems direct-

COHORTS

ly from my continuing association with Ed du Moulin. His wide perspective and his quiet strength are mighty and enduring influences on lives that they touch.

Andy MacGowan

Ed du Moulin is the quintessential "people person." Imagine working your way up from a $7-a-week go-fer at Basche & Co. all the way to Board Vice-Chairman without selling a single share of stock! Ed doesn't think of himself as a salesman, but I know better. I have seen Ed sell his ideas to some real tough people.

He has demonstrated time and again that he can come up with very good advice, then convince people to follow up and get things done with great focus. I have seen him raise millions of dollars for a cause he believes in. And Ed never forgets a thing. With these attributes, it's no wonder he has been a terrific America's Cup manager.

Another reason for Ed's success and popularity is that he loves his family, and has a large extended one. Even so, he always seems to have time for everyone, whether that time is spent getting a stray's life back on track, managing an

America's Cup effort, working hard for a good cause, or giving sound advice.

I appreciate how fortunate I am to have Ed in my life. He is a huge factor in whatever success I may have had on the water, but he has also been, and continues to be, a wonderful friend, through thick and thin. I am sure this lets you know that I really love him, and I know I am only one of many who feel this way.

I know you will enjoy reading some of Ed's recollections on three decades of America's Cup lore.

Dennis Conner

AUTHOR'S NOTE

What I have written is factual and truthful, but does represent my side of what were sometimes highly controversial and convoluted situations. Those who might not agree with my representations are entitled to their viewpoints. I respect their right to disagree.

In spite of the ever-growing intrusion, and I feel it is an intrusion, of commercialism as well as the proliferation of "hired guns" crossing national boundaries, the America's Cup is alive and well. After 150 years (2001) it continues to be a seriously contested, international sports classic – a challenge for national supremacy – providing an ego trip for some, but a true crusade for others.

These chapters are not a comprehensive history of the Cup. Rather, they are simply small segments of a subject thoroughly covered by hundreds of other books, starting with Lawson's *History of the America's Cup*

(1851 - 1900), ending with Dennis Conner's *The America's Cup – The History of Sailing's Greatest Competition in the Twentieth Century* and with some of the more noteworthy mentioned herein.

Were it not for my special and most missed daughter Cathy and her husband Jerry Morea, I never would have undertaken writing these memoirs. Their gift of an old computer provided a learning experience as well as the machinery necessary.

Roger Vaughan was working with Gary Jobson filming the Knickerbocker Cup in New York when Eleanor and I stopped to have a chat with him. Roger encouraged me to write my America's Cup memoirs. He has been of invaluable help, and has my gratitude, as does his wife, editor Kippy Requardt.

The proceeds from the sale of this book will go to the Herreshoff Marine Museum's America's Cup Hall of Fame in Bristol, Rhode Island.

8

ELEANOR C. DU MOULIN
(1921 – 2000)

"An Induction Ceremony, with all the surrounding pomp and circumstance, is an occasion to reflect on the remarkable achievements of individuals. Such is the case this year with induction of Ed du Moulin. Yet it is hard to think of Ed without his closest of friends, his companion, his wife of 58 years, Eleanor. Eleanor was a very special person, beloved by a whole generation of America's Cup crew members. Her 'joie de vie' lit up every occasion, and her great charm had an infectious effect on all who met her.

"Many an America's Cup sailor will recount the warm and nurturing role Eleanor played in so many of those long and hard-fought Cup efforts. Then, elation was often mixed with years of deflation but always Eleanor was present to support and give strength, not only to Ed, but to all involved.

"I saw Eleanor at the announcement of this year's inductees at a function in New York City in June. She was, as always, radiant. Proud of her husband's achievements yet totally selfless in her demeanor, Eleanor graced that occasion. This celebration today is in part a tribute to Eleanor du Moulin."

Halsey Herreshoff
Herreshoff Marine Museum
America's Cup Hall of Fame
Induction Ceremony, September 17, 2000

CHAPTER 1

LEARNING

y interest in the America's Cup began when I had the opportunity to sail to Block Island in 1937 on Sam Lauterbach's 45-foot yawl *Thora*. I was 23. My father, a Wall Street lawyer, had died in the flu epidemic of 1919. My mother brought up my sister, brother and me. Sam Lauterbach had come into our lives during my high school days. A bachelor cousin, he was a fine sailor and skier, and he introduced me to these wonderful sports as well as to the America's Cup.

That year was the swan song of the fantastic J-boats. The defense was to be held off Newport, Rhode Island. Harold "Mike" Vanderbilt was the skipper of the defender *Ranger*. Thomas Sopwith was challenging in *Endeavour II*. With excitement and curiosity, I had read every book I could find on the history surrounding this great trophy.

I was already familiar with the stories about the famous yacht designers Olin and Rod Stephens. My first exposure to the Stephens brothers had been an unforgettable evening (circa 1936) at the Princeton Club. Rod had given a talk, along with movies, about *Stormy Weather*'s transatlantic victory in the race to Norway. I carry to this day his vivid description of how the skipper of *Hamrah* was lost overboard during a storm. Several of his sons jumped in to save him. All perished.

While on Block Island in 1937, Cousin Sam presented me with a package containing small teak models of *Endeavour II* and *Ranger*, with metal masts and sails, wind arrow and a buoy tilted at the bottom to depict current direction. The set was manufactured by the Herreshoff Manufacturing Company of Bristol, Rhode Island. It was meant to be used by protest committees, and for teaching sailing fundamentals. When the Herreshoff Marine Museum was established, I

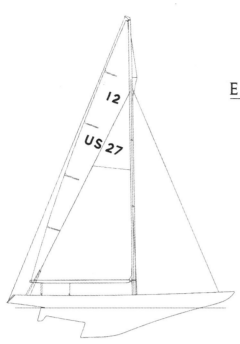

1977

ENTERPRISE SYNDICATE

CHAIRMAN
G.F. Jewett, Jr.

GENERAL MANAGER
Ed du Moulin

SKIPPER
Lowell North
Malin Burnham

DESIGNER
Sparkman & Stephens

BUILDER
Minneford's

described this set to Halsey Herreshoff who was positive that the HM Co. never had made such a product. I sent the set to him. It can be seen today in the Herreshoff Marine Museum.

The history of the Herreshoffs of Bristol was also familiar to me back in 1937. But I never dreamed that one day I would become a close friend of Halsey Herreshoff, and figure quite so prominently in the development of the Marine Museum's America's Cup Hall of Fame. It all seemed so glamorous and out of reach. Just goes to show that life can provide some amazing twists and turns.

Returning to the 1937 Cup engagement: the one race that stands out in my memory took place on a day when the fog was thick as pea soup. The course was 15 miles to windward, 15 miles to leeward. A good breeze was blowing. We decided to leave our Block Island mooring on *Thora* and sail to a spot where we figured the J's would pass on the downwind leg. We followed the radio reports and patiently sailed back and forth. Suddenly, a Coast Guard cutter appeared out of the fog and ordered us out of the way – a race was in progress. Our captain yelled back in his native German. This delaying tactic worked.

We were treated, a few minutes later, to a truly awe-inspiring sight: out of the fog appeared *Ranger*'s 18,000 square foot spinnaker. As any seaman knows, an object suddenly appearing out of a dense fog appears to be much larger than it actually is. And a J-class yacht is quite impressive enough without the added apparent magnification.

We enjoyed an equally amazing close-up view of *Ranger*, her afterguard and crew as the boat passed us and re-entered the fog bank. A few moments later, we were lucky enough to witness the same breath-taking view of the magnificent blue-hulled *Endeavour II*. To this day these memories give me a great thrill.

With war clouds gathering, it was quite natural for me to join the U.S. Coast Guard. From August, 1941, through October, 1945, I served in the Offshore Anti-Submarine Patrol, and on Atlantic Coast and Mediterranean convoy duty. Then in 1945, I was back at my job with J. S. Bache & Co., an old Wall Street brokerage firm, and once again able to go sailing. I enjoyed a fairly successful racing experience on Long Island Sound as well as racing to Bermuda. My son Richard sailed with me from the age of three. I renewed my interest, albeit at a distance, in Cup campaigns in 1958, that being the first postwar defense.

In 1967, this changed when Richard, while at Dartmouth, was recruited by Emil "Bus" Mosbacher and Robert McCullough of the New York Yacht Club to sail on *Constellation* as a tailer. *Constellation*, a contender, was skippered by Bob McCullough and *Intrepid*, the ultimately successful defender, was under the command of Bus Mosbacher. This was my first direct connection with the Cup. That summer my wife Eleanor and I watched much of the trials from a discreet parental distance. One evening Eleanor and I were guests at the crew house. The formality was impressive. I had the opportunity to discuss with Olin Stephens my thoughts concerning a design for a 38-foot "Pilot" with the underbody of *Intrepid*, trim tab and all. This resulted in the Hinckley 38.

Richard's credentials, besides sailing with me and racing one-designs, included a number of Bermuda races beginning with our first Bermuda Race together, in 1966, on board E. Bates McKee's "slow boat to China," *Xanadu II*. Richard sailed his first transatlantic race to Germany on *Ondine* when he was 17 with his sailing buddy John Browning. Later, as a naval officer, he served three years as Ocean Racing Coach at the Naval Academy.

Then in the 1974 defense, Richard was invited to become navigator on *Mariner*. The syndicate manager was George Hinman, a past commodore of the New York Yacht Club, and a close neighbor of ours. *Mariner*'s skipper was Ted Turner, with Dennis Conner as his tactician. Britton Chance was the designer. During the construction and early training sessions, some of *Mariner*'s crew stayed with us in Sands Point, Long Island. They made themselves at home, leaving our house early for Bob Derecktor's boatyard in Mamaroneck, New York, and very often returning late in the evening, tired and in need of showers. They pitched in with the kitchen chores. Eleanor and I very much enjoyed what might have been considered by some to have been the confusion of having these energetic house-guests. This turned out to be a foretaste of our subsequent and very happy experiences living under the same roof with our America's Cup crews.

Otherwise, this was to be a summer of horrors for those who sailed on the red

M. Tank tests proved to be fallible, resulting in a mid-season hull rebuild, much frustration, and loss of valuable sailing time. Ultimately, *Mariner* was eliminated. Dennis, who had for a short period replaced Turner as *Mariner*'s skipper, was invited to join the Ted Hood-skippered Courageous as starting helmsman/tactician, while Richard was invited by Gerry Driscoll to be navigator on *Intrepid*. He would be a shipmate with Andy MacGowan. Andy and Rich would later be responsible for my playing a much more active role in the Cup.

Eleanor and I closely followed the trials, which have to go down in Cup history as some of the most closely fought. On the very last day of the final trials *Courageous* eliminated *Intrepid*. (Read *The Grand Gesture* by Roger Vaughan for the full story.)

During the *Courageous* construction period, Olin Stephens, her designer, met with me. The syndicate was short of funds; construction had stopped. He asked if I would contact Rear Admiral Sheldon Kinney, head of the New York Maritime College, Ft. Schuyler, New York about the possibility of establishing a foundation through which syndicate supporters could make tax deductible donations. Admiral Kinney, understandably, said a foundation could not be established in time to be meaningful, but he could see the possibilities for the future. Fortunately, Syndicate Head Bob McCullough stepped into the financial breach, allowing the *Courageous* construction to continue.

The meeting with the admiral turned out to be the beginning of a wonderful relationship. In 1976, the Maritime College at Ft. Schuyler Foundation was established. I was asked to serve on the board of trustees which included names familiar to the sailing world: Julian Roosevelt, F. Briggs Dalzell, Charles Ulmer among others. I retired from the board 20 gratifying years later, leaving the Foundation alive and well, and continuing to support the College and its cadets.

In 1974, after 41 years, I had retired from Bache, as Vice-Chairman of the Board, except for special duties as a director. In 1975, with *Intrepid*'s near victory on their minds, two enthusiastic crew members, Andrew MacGowan and my son Richard, approached me. They urged me to become manager of a new syndicate for the next (1977) defense of the America's Cup. Their proposal was simple. With my managerial experience and the substantial backing of George F. Jewett, Jr., the syndicate would be a natural.

I was faced with a case of reverse nepotism. My son was recruiting me, not the usual case of father introducing son into the fold. And in all modesty, looking back over the *Enterprise* years, this never became an issue.

George "Fritz" Jewett and his wife Lucy, from San Francisco, had been the major backers and inspiration for the 1974 *Intrepid* campaign. Although Richard had been part of their team, I had never met this wonderful couple. They were responsible for the involvement of the Seattle Sailing Foundation as a vehicle through which funds could be raised to finance an America's Cup campaign. To justify the tax exemption, a foundation must be left with substantial assets to be used for the purposes set forth in the exemption. The Seattle Sailing Foundation was one of the first tax exempt foundations to be used by a Cup syndicate. The Kings Point Fund of the U.S. Merchant Marine Academy was, I believe, the very first to establish such a foundation a few years earlier.

Before agreeing to take on the management of a Cup campaign, I visited George Hinman, then chairman of the America's Cup Committee, whom I knew and greatly respected. Commodore Hinman certainly had experienced more than his fair share of frustrations as both manager and skipper of various contenders. He thought my managing a syndicate was a great idea, and he made the point that managing a syndicate was not overly complicated. (After my subsequent experiences in this regard, I would make this point: don't you believe it.) I asked Commodore Hinman if he would allow me to approach his personal counsel and advisor, Harman Hawkins, to seek his guidance. Hinman quickly approved. What a wonderful break for me and a lot of hard work for the ever busy Harman.

Harman Hawkins proved to be invaluable in the organizing of our program, in our relations with the Maritime College at Ft. Schuyler Foundation, and in keeping us out of trouble. All this was pro bono, and in spite of a desk loaded with other interests. What an invaluable contribution. Harman would also serve in that important role in the 1980 and 1983 campaigns and would be closely involved with me in the 1988 catamaran controversy.

The next step was for me to meet with the Jewetts, Admiral Kinney, and Olin Stephens to decide if we should move ahead as a syndicate. We met in September, 1975, at New York's Kennedy Airport. The meeting went exceedingly well. We seemed to be a compatible group, so we shook hands and agreed to form a syndicate. We had experience, character and leadership on our side. All to the good. We would meet again, to discuss the actual organization, a budget, and fund raising. Meanwhile, Admiral Kinney called a meeting of the Ft. Schuyler Foundation trustees to obtain their approval.

Archibald Cox, Jr., a managing director of Morgan Stanley, the investment bankers, was a popular and able sailor. I invited him to meet with Admiral Kinney, Harman Hawkins and myself, at the Manhasset Bay Yacht Club. We discussed the outline of our syndicate plans and asked Archie if he would lead our vital fund raising efforts. As cautious as any successful banker should be, he said he would make his decision after he met with the Jewetts.

Prior to any of these meetings, Richard had given me a copy of a speech he had given in 1975 before the Chesapeake Sailing Yacht Symposium in Annapolis. It was called "America's Cup 1974 – An Overview."

This document included cost breakdowns of the three 1974 contending syndicates. They ranged from $800,000 for *Intrepid* to $1,250,000 for *Courageous*. It was from these figures I established an initial budget for our syndicate of $1,500,000. The increase allowed for inflation, for an elaborate model testing program (the first to use one-third scale models), and for a special sail development study. We had lost confidence in the smaller models used in developing the ill-fated Britton Chance design in 1974.

I would like to quote Richard's conclusion from the Symposium speech:

"My objective has been not to criticize or condemn, but rather to acquaint the sailing public with the challenges both on and off the race course. A 12–meter effort is far more than just crew practice and an eight-second spinnaker set. It is truly a test of leadership, management, fund raising, steering, tactics, crew work, design, construction, tuning, and sailmaking."

Given my son's clarity of thought, you cannot say I was not forewarned.

With the potential for a very strong syndicate team, a skipper had to be chosen on whose shoulders the ultimate responsibility would be placed to "win on the water." I listed 20 of the biggest names in yacht racing. The list, of course, included Dennis Conner and Ted Turner. After many discussions, among the Enterprise Committee members, we selected Lowell North who not only had prior 12-meter experience, but an astonishing success on the racing circuit. He had been outstanding as a Star World Champion, he had distinguished himself in the SORC, and he had created North Sails. He was looked up to by other world-class sailors.

The Enterprise Committee included Archie Cox as vice-chairman (he had met and been impressed with the Jewetts – and vice versa); Admiral Kinney, of course, representing the Maritime College; Fritz Jewett; and myself as chairman/manager. Although I carried the title of chairman, I have no problem acknowledging that it was Fritz Jewett who was the real chairman of the board.

I called Lowell, and he agreed to be skipper. Lowell, as we got to know him, was a modest, kind, and decent person. He simply had his own way of doing things. He proved to be a true scientist and would often lose himself in his experiments. As we found out, he was not a strong hands-on leader. Had we been aware of these shortcomings, we very likely might not have picked him. We didn't do our homework in depth. It was only when Dennis Conner joined us to lead the Freedom campaign, in 1980, that we learned Dennis had been disappointed in not being asked to skipper *Enterprise*. Our reasons for not considering either Ted Turner or Dennis had been based on questions of overt personality incompatibilities. Certainly Lowell had just as good a reputation as either as a successful competitor. Such is life...

After a number of winter practices in San Diego, doubt was raised about Lowell's leadership by several of the crew as well as by my psychic wife Eleanor. However, I remained confident that someone with his outstanding accomplishments could handle Ted Turner and Ted Hood on the water.

Our competing defense syndicate was led by A. Lee Loomis, an important New York Yacht Club member, former owner of the 12-meter *Northern Light*, and successful investment leader. He was aptly called the "Big Loom." He took on the formidable job of having Ted Turner as skipper of the battle-tested *Courageous*, and Ted Hood as skipper of a newly built 12-meter, *Independence*. It was well accepted that Loomis favored the quiet Hood to the outspoken Turner, but Loomis weathered all the storms, and to his credit came out on top.

uring this period, the Kings Point Fund, the funding entity for Loomis' syndicate, was facing some problems with the IRS. The most publicized one related to a complex transaction involving a gift of stock, and the fund receiving the replica of the yacht *America*. After considerable legal expense to the fund and a large settlement against the donor, the matter was settled. Thanks to Harman Hawkins and our foundation's counsel, we never ran into any such problems.

Late into December of 1976, Turner and Hood practiced in Marblehead, sometimes in snowy conditions, giving them a head start. Campaigns had rarely been active on the water more than five months ahead of the Cup races. This new and ambitious schedule prompted us to send *Enterprise* to San Diego and secure *Intrepid* as a trial horse.

In 1980, Dennis Conner was accused of being the first to initiate a two-season campaign. In reality, it was started by the Turner/Hood syndicate with their winter practice. This turned out to be step-one in a major escalation of the Cup preparation period.

Intrepid was an asset a southwestern bank had acquired through a default. It was a most complicated negotiation to purchase her for our syndicate's use as a trial horse. William Dalessi of the Long Beach Yacht Club, a highly reputable lawyer, volunteered to help us obtain legal possession of *Intrepid*. He asked my son

Richard, who was in the shipping business, to help with the negotiations.

The members of the San Diego Yacht Club, from which so many of the world's best sailors have come (Malin Burnham, Dennis Conner, Gerry Driscoll, Lowell North…), welcomed us with open arms. They housed many of our crew (and families), entertained us, provided a first class race committee, created office space, and made our crew lunches. Many of the friendships established then are still going strong. Few imagined that 10 years later the America's Cup would be theirs to defend.

Let's go back a bit. One vital meeting still had to be held before actually moving ahead with the Enterprise Syndicate. After all, the New York Yacht Club held the America's Cup and our syndicate would be representing them. The club had to approve our program. As a member of the NYYC, I arranged for a luncheon meeting at the clubhouse to be attended by members of the America's Cup Committee which, as I recall, included Commodores Robert McCullough, George Hinman, and Harry Anderson, Jr., among others. Our group included the Jewetts, Admiral Kinney, Archie Cox, and Olin Stephens. The Jewetts flew in from San Francisco. I had prepared an agenda. The only opportunity to discuss it with Fritz Jewett was in the men's room of the club. We quickly agreed on the procedure to follow. It was at this meeting that Archie Cox first met the Jewetts, and came on board. After a fascinating meeting, the Cup Committee gave the Enterprise Syndicate its blessing. We were on the way.

Between 1974 and 1976, Halsey Herreshoff (already a veteran of several Cup campaigns), Richard du Moulin (*Intrepid*'s navigator in the later stage of the 1974 campaign), and Dick McCurdy (a super electronics expert) had worked on an instrument package for the upcoming defense. In one of my first phone conversations with Lowell, I mentioned this to him, fully expecting he would be glad to study it. To my surprise and disappointment, Lowell said he was not interested. He had his own special ideas. I decided not to argue since this was the first issue to arise. After all, he was the skipper and had to be satisfied with his equipment.

As it turned out, the instrument package used on *Enterprise* never worked effectively. It was jokingly said that Lowell spent more time up the mast, adjusting his sophisticated instruments, than he did in the cockpit.

Crew recruitment was no problem. Lowell, with Andy MacGowan's help, selected some veterans from the 1974 Intrepid campaign who were to become the backbone of an excellent crew. Most important was the recruitment of cadets from the Maritime College. We believed this would substantiate our relationship with the foundation, and benefit all involved. There were hundreds of young men and some women who were interested in volunteering their services. Applications were carefully reviewed. Attitude was a basic requirement, and experience was not always required. Over the years, I learned you could take a raw candidate and mold him into a first-class crew. In most instances, the crew itself would screen out those who might not "cut the mustard" over a long, hard campaign.

During the early winter of 1977 in California, Lowell concentrated on boat speed. He would sail long distances against *Intrepid* (with Gerry Driscoll, her skipper in 1974, at the helm) working on boat speed and sail trim. The *Enterprise* crew were not happy sitting quietly on these long test runs. They wanted a chance to practice tacking, spinnaker handling and other drills against *Intrepid*. On one of these days I went along. Both 12's sailed off to the south on one long tack. Suddenly, I realized we were in Mexican waters. As manager, and thus being responsible for the program, I worried that our insurance might not cover sailing in foreign waters. We turned back north. Upon checking, it turned out that we were in fact covered "South of the Border." To encourage more crew work during these sailing sessions, I decided to be on board more often.

Being on board a 12-meter was a great way to remind me that the Cup would be won or lost on the water. I was an interested passenger/observer, never throwing my weight around. The boat was the domain of the skipper and crew. It was particularly exciting to sail with Dennis or Jack Sutphen in later campaigns when they raced hard against each other. Often I would handle a running backstay – not always perfectly – except when sailing with Sutphen. My main objective would be to keep out of the way. It was always comforting to watch, at close hand, the enthusiasm and ability of the crew. My only sailing in Newport during those years would be on the 12s. My 39-foot Carter *Blaze* was at the compound, but I never relaxed long enough to sail her. It became a floating hotel for family and friends. Later, I donated her to the Maritime Foundation.

Lowell had a relaxed California style, and he certainly did have excellent boat-handling skills. One day, we left the San Diego Yacht Club for a practice without a tender. He calmly sailed away from the dock. Hard to imagine that happening today. Much to my concern he took *Enterprise* well offshore, our only escort some very nearby whales. It was customary to have a boat escort in attendance in case of emergency. On returning to the SDYC, Lowell made a picture-perfect landing without outside assistance. Lowell didn't do this to show off. It was a normal and natural action. I was impressed. Nevertheless, I told him that he must take a tender with him in the future. *Enterprise* was the property of the Maritime Foundation and we were responsible for her safety, as well as that of the crew.

After the winter in San Diego, we trailered *Enterprise* back to Newport, Rhode Island. We were fortunate to be able to secure an old mansion called Seaview

Terrace as our crew home thanks once again to Andy MacGowan, our procurer. It was owned by the brother of former Governor Carey of New York. We were permitted to use 30 of its 62 rooms. During the school year, it served as a dormitory for Salve Regina College. Far from being in top condition, it did have ample grounds and facilities for drying sails, for crew parties, for physical training, and the other stretch-out needs of an America's Cup campaign. To improve the quality of basic dorm life, Eleanor and Roberta Burnham purchased cheap but decorative bed sheets and hung them up as draperies. Mary Walsh, a friend to all Cup families, trucked over old paintings and lamps. Among the properties Mary owned was Castle Hill, overlooking Newport harbor entrance, and which had been aptly dubbed "Mildew Manor" by an earlier America's Cup crew.

Our ladies of Seaview Terrace were an outstanding group, and everyone got along beautifully. Kay North gave wonderful haircuts to the crew. The fun-loving Lucy Jewett set a fast and lively pace. They certainly helped make it a home for the crew and their families and were superb hostesses for our many guests.

Each morning before the crew left for the compound, our very good friend, Dr. Howard Browne, would come to Seaview Terrace to check out any crew health problems. This was a labor of love on his part, and would continue through our other Newport campaigns. So many donated so much, and all were so appreciated.

At the time, we didn't realize that the experience of living together under these conditions throughout a strenuous Cup program was destined to change quite drastically after the *Freedom*-1980 defense. Already, we were seeing alterations in what had been the norm. Prior to 1977, protocol in an America's Cup crew house was definitely more formal. Dinner attendance was mandatory as were jackets and ties. We at the *Enterprise* house were about to be introduced to the "California style." Our group opted for a little less formal dinner attire: sport shirts.

Lowell informed me that a jacuzzi was en route from San Diego by truck. I didn't know what a jacuzzi was. Stories began to circulate about nude, mixed company, and nocturnal bathing forays, sometimes all elements together. What would the staid NYYC's America's Cup Committee have to say about this? We prepared for the worst. But no problems arose, perhaps because an enterprising *Enterprise* crew member decided to drop a few lobsters in the tank. This cooled the ardor of future guests, particularly the ladies, for the glories of the jacuzzi.

It was standard policy to have "house rules" which specified a fairly early curfew. Most of the time the crew was too tired from a very long day to jump ship. Bus Mosbacher, when he was campaigning, had been able to hear his crew returning late by the noise made when they walked on the gravel driveway. Aside from periodic curfew jumping by some of our sailors who managed ingenious ways of departing and even more ingenious ways of returning (often by the fire escape), we had minimum trouble. It is quite astonishing by today's standards to realize how responsible we felt for the crew and their families.

Only one domestic incident stands out. A crewman had a longstanding relationship with a very pretty girl. She became involved with one of his shipmates, which led to a dangerous confrontation that I witnessed. Our jilted crewman picked up either an axe or sledge to flatten out his "enemy." It reached the point where one of them would have to leave the syndicate. Both were important members of the crew. I chickened out of making that decision and handed it to Dave Pedrick, a young designer assigned by Sparkman & Stephens to work full time on our project. I asked Dave if he would lead a crew discussion and advise me as to which of the two antagonists the crew, as a group, thought they might best do without. I was concerned that if I did it, the crew might be intimidated. It all worked as planned and resulted in a quiet departure. Years later, I received a thoughtful letter of apology from the dismissed individual. He had married the girl.

I did discover that much of a syndicate manager's time is taken away from solving sailing issues and spent solving social problems. Our larger contributors had to be carefully handled. At the same time, it was important not to slight the many smaller contributors (of which we had a record number), friends, and local VIPs. Matters such as upon whose spectator boats should we dispatch which of our guests required careful attention. We had to be sensitive to the wishes of the owners of the yachts who permitted us to place guests aboard.

In one instance, an aged owner wanted the "girl from California in the shorty-shorts" assigned as a guest aboard his yacht. However, his lady friend (later his wife) ordered, in no uncertain terms, that I was not to permit "*that*" girl on board. I didn't.

On another occasion, I was informed that the commodore of the San Diego Yacht Club had been rudely treated by a major backer whose yacht was tied to our 12-meter pier. The commodore came over to our dockside via rubber boat from Goat Island to pay his respects. As he climbed up the bulkhead ladder, he was unceremoniously confronted by our syndicate member who, thinking he was a spy, chased him off the dock.

Insulting the commodore of the San Diego Yacht Club that had been so good to us the winter before could not be passed over lightly. Obtaining a sincere apology from our unofficial "guard" was not too difficult, but placating the injured party turned out to be a real challenge.

One of my truly bothersome responsibilities was to balance the interests of the Foundation which owned our equipment, the New York Yacht Club for whom we were sailing, and the major financial supporters who controlled the necessary funding. Walking such a tightrope was not new to me, but required careful consideration nonetheless. An example: the major financial backers felt they should name the boat. Naturally, the Yacht Club felt it had an interest, but it was the Foundation that actually owned the vessel. I made sure Admiral Kinney had the last word.

After the winter practice was over, we sold *Intrepid* in California for a substantially higher price than what we had paid. This was then questioned by the bankruptcy lawyers who had handled the original sale. Had we paid them a fair price? We easily justified the added value, having subsequently commissioned the Driscoll Shipyard to restore *Intrepid* to a competitive condition.

We had determined that our budget could not support bringing a second boat to Newport. This would have required a second crew, additional housing, food, insurance, shipyard expenses. The NYYC had been anxious to have *Intrepid* come east and be a fourth boat in the defender trials. We, however, stuck to our guns and our pocketbook.

One day, I was invited to appear before the America's Cup Committee. Chairman Hinman informed me that Gerry Driscoll was ready to bring *Intrepid* east, and that he only needed an additional $35,000. The chairman said that his committee would raise that sum. I was taken by surprise. No one had spoken to our group about this proposal. I quietly explained that we had no plans to bring a second boat to Newport; that it would cost well upwards of $100,000 additional to campaign another boat, what with the doubled costs of maintenance and crew. These items were not in our budget. The matter was immediately dropped.

From the beginning, with the guidance of Sparkman & Stephens, we had planned a special tank testing program using a 23-foot (one-third) scale model. This was a first. After the *Mariner* episode, we were leery about the smaller models. We also planned a unique sail study to be conducted by Lowell and his North Sails loft.

The sail study led to a frustrating and ultimately unsolvable disagreement. Ted Turner believed he had a promise from Lowell to make sails for him. The "promise" was made "across the water" during an earlier regatta and before Lowell was asked to be our skipper. When we initiated our special sail research program it was, of course, to be exclusive to our syndicate – after all, we were paying for it. But Ted never let up, and succeeded in making Lowell's life miserable by publicly accusing him of going back on his word. It almost led to a fistfight at our syndicate party. The NYYC upheld our argument. North Sails was to make the best sails they could for our competitors, but without input from our special program.

In Long Beach for the 1977 Congressional Cup, I had breakfast with Ted in the hope that I could get him to see our viewpoint. Not a chance. He would not give an inch, nor would I. Our famous revolutionary "green garbage bag" synthetic sail was lighter and could be used in a greater range of wind conditions. However, of itself, it failed to turn the Turner tide. The synthetic sail would be the sail of the future. Lowell, the scientist, was on the right track.

Protocol calls for an American defense contender, when eliminated, to offer its equipment, including sails, to the ultimate defender, to present as strong a defense as possible. But during the trials each individual group must do its very best to outdo its opponents. The intensity of each contender's determination to beat his opponent, to win the right to defend, is the ingredient that led to so many successful defenses.

rom the outset of our campaign we made every effort to establish a fully cooperative relationship with the Maritime Foundation. We had no intention of merely using it as a convenient conveyance for our donated funds. Admiral Kinney assigned their Waterfront Director, Lt. Cmdr. Richard Chesebrough to work with me. We wanted to recruit cadets (undergraduates) to help operate our support boats and give them the opportunity to try out for crew positions.

"Chese" did an outstanding job in selecting cadets to join our program. Over three subsequent Cup campaigns we enjoyed the benefit of their contributions to our programs, and enjoyed having them on board. Cadets like Bill Trenkle, Scott Vogel, and Tom Rich became household names in the yachting world. Dick Chesebrough became our chase boat operator through the Freedom and Australian campaigns. His participation was a real labor of love. He was a hustler who knew only one speed – full ahead.

All of us involved in our three America's Cup syndicates (1977, 1980 and 1983) were there as volunteers. The fact that the campaigns, from 1958 through 1983, were conducted by amateur skippers and crews (our crew received $75 monthly spending money), and folks like the Chesebroughs, helped keep the budgets so much smaller than future campaigns. Dorothea (Dot) Chesebrough, like our other ladies, pitched in too. I remember when Dot helped run the Stars & Stripes retail store in Australia. What a bonanza that was – the more S&S won, the more we sold. One customer drove up in a limo and bought several thousand dollars of our merchandise.

Volunteers Bob and Ann Conner of Newport, Rhode Island, were also so important and so helpful to us. Bob, who was with Raytheon, secured valuable and important electronic equipment for us, and as importantly, helped us maintain it. The Conners also set up weather instruments on the roof of their home by the ocean, which fed data to our tender and 12-meter.

Fund raising required a good deal of research and follow through. Once we began collecting for the *Enterprise* effort, I visited the Model Room of the NYYC, surely a yachting wonder of the world. I copied the names of the various living syndicate members from the brass plaques next to each model defender. The next job was to obtain proper introductions to these evidently interested, generous people. One example was the late Charles Payson.

A luncheon meeting was arranged through Commodore McCullough. We explained the background of our syndicate to Mr. Payson, after which he agreed to make a generous donation. Sometime later, I received a call from an irate Lee Loomis, the outspoken leader of the Turner-Hood syndicate. "How come you misled Mr. Payson?" When Mr. Loomis approached Mr. Payson, the latter said he had already committed to Commodore McCullough's syndicate. Of course, it was not McCullough's syndicate as Payson had assumed. The problem was solved when Mr. Payson committed an equal amount to the Loomis group. In 1980, Loomis joined our Freedom campaign. On occasion, Dennis Conner, *Freedom*'s skipper, would invite "The Big Loom" on board. He would spread himself out on the transom and offer his observations to Dennis, who always listened.

Although the bulk of our funds came from a relatively few major donors, we diligently and appreciatively cultivated every possible source. We had over 500 individual contributors from throughout the nation, a record number. Over 90 percent of our money came from private individuals, less than 10 percent from corporations. By contrast, it's worth noting that after the loss of the Cup in 1983, about 90 percent of our dollars came from corporations. Thus entered a new era in the history of the Cup. I personally was much saddened to see the glory days go by.

Shortly after the announcement of the *Enterprise* project, I received a phone call in my home office. I was working with Andy MacGowan. From his racing experience, which started with me on my Pilot *Lady Del*, his working at Sparkman & Stephens, and his time spent crewing aboard the 12-meters *Weatherly* and *Intrepid*, Andy had an excellent grasp of what products we would need for a campaign. The phone call I received went something like this: "This is J. Patrick Moran, Jr. I am a member of the NYYC and would like to help." I replied that our main need was money, not volunteers. He said he would send us $100 (which he did). We gave him a polite brush-off. His calls kept coming in, until one day, at Andy's suggestion, we gave Patrick a long list of material we would like to obtain, as contributions-in-kind, from corporations around the country. We thought this was one sure way of getting rid of him. For several weeks, we heard nothing. Suddenly, packages began to be delivered which we stored in my shed – from

23

sandpaper to toilet paper; tools, life jackets, toothpaste, outboard motors, a very wide range of supplies. Patrick had talked Paul Stuart, a high-end clothier, into a commitment to supply our dress uniforms. For three campaigns, the Patrick-generated flow never stopped. Patrick maintained close contact with his suppliers during our 1977 campaign thus ensuring that they would help us in future campaigns. These gifts were as good as cash and helped keep our budget under control.

Later, Patrick became publisher of the America's Cup Challenge magazine. He was assisting the current New York Yacht Club Year 2000 challenge until his untimely death in December, 1997. I shall not forget J. Patrick Moran, Jr.

Of special importance to the Enterprise syndicate was William Foulk, Jr., who served on many NYYC race committees and was an experienced sailor. Bill was invaluable on the bridge of Briggs Cunningham's *Chaperone*, our tender. One very foggy day, *Enterprise* was racing *Courageous*. My son Richard had hurt his back, and asked Halsey Herreshoff to pinch hit for him as navigator.

On board *Chaperone*, Bill was following a large ship on our radar. It seemed likely that it would cross the path of the 12s. Just at the moment *Enterprise* approached the fog-shrouded turning buoy, the dim outline of the ship was sighted. Bill raised an arm, pointed, and called, "There it is."

Upon returning to our dock, Bill and I were summoned by the Cup Committee. We thought we were going to be congratulated for Halsey's fine navigation. Bill was called in first. Shortly, he exited with a shocked look. I was immediately ushered in to what turned out to be a confrontation. The remark as to the position of the ship had been heard by Commodore Mosbacher riding the nearby Cup Committee's powerboat. We were accused of pointing out the turning mark to *Enterprise*. I was stunned, and strongly denied this. No way would Bill or I commit such an indiscretion.

That afternoon there was to be a cocktail party given by the Cup Committee, to which Eleanor and I had been invited. I was reluctant to go but Eleanor insisted. To my surprise, and I might say gratification, members of the Committee quietly apologized to me for the accusation.

On the lighter side, Eleanor who was on a spectator yacht with Becky Herreshoff, Halsey's 90-year-old mother, told us that Becky criticized Halsey for not making the mark on the nose. When first spotted, the mark had been less than 100 yards away. But Becky expected a Herreshoff to be perfect.

Another valuable volunteer was Dick Walling, a 12-meter veteran. He always had suggestions, and would put his money where his mouth was. In 1977, our grinders complained that our genoa sheets were slipping. Dick offered to fly the winch drums to a steel mill and have them coated with a special abrasive. He heli-coptered them back a few days later. But now the genny sheets were breaking under strain as a result of the overly abrasive drums. Undaunted, Dick restored the winches to their previous configuration, footing the bill of $5,000.

John Dorrance, Jr., Chairman of the Campbell Soup Company, was a long-time supporter of NYYC defenses. He was one of the most humble men I ever met. His yacht was tied up to our pier. One day, he noticed that the *Enterprises*'s winches were not the new self-tailers. He insisted we take, and keep, his new winches. He would use our outdated ones.

At the time of Lowell's replacement as skipper, I was under heavy pressure. The America's Cup Committee was upset about a remark of Lowell's which appeared in a New York paper after his removal. He was quoted as saying that he hoped Australia would win the Cup. I had to caution Lowell, who was understand-ably quite unhappy given the awkward attention he was receiving from all sides.

Then one afternoon, along came Mr. Dorrance, making a rare appearance in our trailer office. This will be just the last straw if *he* has a complaint, I was think-ing. Without a word, he placed an envelope on my desk and left. Inside was a size-able check with a note saying that he appreciated the dedication of our crew in the face of the discouraging outlook. He was impressed with our active use of the Maritime cadets and the benefits that were accruing to the foundation. What a fine gentleman he was.

But before our prospects were quite so bleak, Lowell had invited Malin Burnham into *Enterprise*'s cockpit as his next in command. Malin is a calm, intelli-gent, successful individual and a fine sailor. At age 17, he was the youngest to ever become Star World Champion. John Marshall, a capable sailor, very bright and strong, filled out the 1977 afterguard. Each had a helm assignment. Lowell would start. Malin would take *Enterprise* upwind, and Marshall downwind. John Ahern, a leading sportswriter from Boston, wrote that this arrangement would not work out. He was right.

Malin preferred a tiller to a wheel, and had an extension fitted onto *Enterprise*'s wheel. He could then sit astride the gunwale. This also meant that before each tack, he would have to step down, alerting the competitor to the pending maneu-ver. Certainly, this was not a fundamental reason for our ultimate defeat, but it proved awkward, to say the least.

We fully intended that our syndicate would be considered a *national* one. However, it too often was referred to as "that West Coast syndicate." Our opposi-tion used this to their advantage, as many East Coast sources of contributions, donations, and supplies shied away. Despite the compelling facts that the New

York Yacht Club and the Ft. Schuyler Foundation were located in the East, the boat was built in the East, the manager and designer were from the East, and the crew was from all over the nation, we never did convince the die-hards that we were not "that West Coast syndicate."

Lowell had a plan for eliminating the competition. He wanted to lose the June trials to defuse the competition, then win the July trials, and "sweep the final series." When our Enterprise Committee learned this, Lowell was told that he should do his best to win every race. When we did not do well in the June series, it was understandably upsetting to our major backers.

During the June trials, on one of my days sailing with Lowell, I found myself ankle deep in water in the cockpit. I called this to Lowell's attention. He explained that they had forgotten to open the cockpit drains, and instructed one of the crew to make a note. Later, Andy MacGowan was cleaning the bottom with a long handled brush and came across an obstacle. It turned out to be an elongated teflon protrusion aptly referred to as a "horse cock" – one of them is now in the custody of the America's Cup Hall of Fame in Bristol, Rhode Island. Lowell, with the help of a crewman, had secretly installed two of these in the cockpit drains during the June trials. They had acted as brakes, and had effectively slowed down *Enterprise*. By the time of the discovery, the June trials were history. Lowell was carrying out *his* plan… Naturally, there was consternation among our senior backers. Some urged a change of skipper, but it was too late as the July trials were about to begin.

There was some exciting racing during the July trials, with *Enterprise* coming out on top. What we failed to notice during the very last race of that series, when *Courageous* beat us, was that she was sporting a new eight-ounce dacron jib. We were satisfied that we had "won" the July trials. Lowell still had confidence in the "garbage bag," the material of the future.

The Cup Committee became frustrated with Lowell. Cup Committee member Briggs Cunningham, skipper of the successful defender *Columbia*, would visit our compound almost every morning following a race day. In his soft-spoken manner, he would urge us to make Lowell cover his opponent. In fact, Lowell often did not follow this standard procedure. He was mostly interested in boat speed. When he served his stint as tactician, with Malin steering upwind, Lowell's mind often would be fixed on boat speed, and not on the competitor. This took its toll on the afterguard. It certainly cost us races.

Early on in San Diego, there had been a great deal of discussion as to how big the fore triangle should be. Olin Stephens tried to convince Lowell that a large fore triangle would be better. However, Lowell insisted that his testing proved the opposite. Lowell got his way. Some on board felt it was a mistake, as it made tacking the jib through a smaller triangle more difficult. In a hard tacking duel, we would lose ground. Lowell in his quiet way would not give an inch. Perhaps John Marshall, who worked for Lowell, was exercising self-interested self-restraint in not being overly critical of his boss. It was not until too late in the game that John let us know of his concern by becoming openly upset about Lowell's control of the cockpit.

Often, before the warning gun, Lowell would be testing sails and/or boat speed. Those of us on the tender would become upset as Lowell would stray from the vicinity of the starting area. The America's Cup Selection Committee also noticed these wanderings, warning us on several occasions, and we took these warning seriously. These were the days when defenders were selected at the pleasure of this committee, after all.

The final trials were about to begin. It was now the time to "do or die." Before we knew what hit us, we found ourselves on the verge of elimination. *Courageous* was outperforming both *Independence* and *Enterprise*. The Cup Committee suggested we take drastic action, as did our backers. The decision was made to replace Lowell. I dreaded this moment. It was understood to be traumatic to be eliminated after one's best efforts on the water in the Trials, but it was just as traumatic – maybe more so – to be replaced as a skipper, after putting your heart and soul into such an intensive program. This was an exception to one of the rules I live by: "A sticker never gets stuck."

Lowell engendered a good bit of hero worship, primarily from those who had known him on the West Coast. One emotional incident illustrates the depth of feeling and regard for him. Our youngest crew member was Rod Davis. Upon learning that Lowell was not to be his skipper any longer, he broke down and sobbed. I went out of my way to make sure Rod fully understood the reasons for this unhappy situation.

Rod Davis has gone on to skipper many Cup contenders, and has had to live through a similarly painful experience himself. In 1992, he was skipper of *New Zealand*, on which he came so very close to eliminating *Il Moro Di Venezia*, only to be removed at the last moment (perhaps foolishly – but that is another story). Today, Rod is one of the world's most experienced America's Cup veterans.

With Lowell's removal, Malin deserved a chance to take over. However, the consensus was to contact Dennis Conner who was in Europe for the Star World Championship. This I did. Dennis understandably turned us down. He didn't want to come in as a "hired gun," which illustrates how very different the world was then. As it was, Dennis won this Star Worlds with five aces, a record that still stands.

After Dennis said no, Malin took command. In spite of a gallant effort, we (and *Independence*) lasted for only a few days. The decision had pretty much been made to select *Courageous*. And what a sad and tearful moment for even the most stoic among the crew when the traditionally austere America's Cup Selection Committee would approach a boat to officially announce its elimination. The "straw hats" shook our hands, thanked us for helping with the defense of the Cup, then dismissed the boat and crew from further participation. The choice of defender by the selection committee would end after the 1983 loss of the Cup to Australia. This old tradition, and a colorful one at that, gave way to clinical tallies and scorekeeping, which have not been without questionable moments (witness the 1992 trials).

But with the selection of *Courageous* it was Ted Turner's day to shine, after his disastrous experience in 1974.

The 1977 Enterprise Syndicate, my initial foray into active participation with defending or challenging for the America's Cup, certainly introduced me to some of the highs and lows of both the sport and of the business.

Up until the 12-meter era (beginning in 1958), an America's Cup campaign was financed primarily by one wealthy individual. A few times a handful of backers joined forces to pool their resources, but as the America's Cup became more of an "open event" and as the costs rose, the handful of backers necessarily increased. With the advent of the tax-exempt foundation, an even larger base came into play.

The bulk of the dollars donated, of course, came from a relatively few interested (and wealthy) individuals. It bothered me that in 1977 the majority of donors to the Enterprise Syndicate (there were 500 of them) were not members of the New York Yacht Club. I felt that each member should, in even a modest way, contribute to their club's defense of the Cup. After several sessions with the NYYC, it was agreed that the entire membership would be assessed a $60 charge to help support the defense. And rather than automatically charging the membership, there was a provision included whereby a member could quietly reject the assessment. The syndicates welcomed this show of support and the actual funds generated.

This was only for one campaign.

Our major donors, those over $50,000, were considered our official Syndicate Members. Their most important perk was the privilege of wearing the Syndicate's blazer patch. Additionally, they would be listed on the brass plaque placed alongside the model of the official defender/challenger in the Model Room of the New York Yacht Club's Manhattan clubhouse.

A popular uniform supplier told me during the Enterprise campaign that an extremely wealthy widow (a very recognizable name) would be sailing from Palm

Beach for Newport on her ninety-five-foot yacht. I arranged for berthing at our compound. On arrival, I was invited on board for a social cocktail. She was bedecked with diamonds. Upon inquiring about wearing the syndicate patch, I advised her that it would require a minimum donation of $50,000. She made it quite clear that was too much. Eventually, she did donate $5,000, which barely covered the cost of her dockage.

Of the seven campaigns in which I was involved with fund raising, the 1977 syndicate would be the only one to have a potential member renege. This man volunteered a donation of $100,000, after which he shook Admiral Kinney's hand. In spite of our best efforts, this potential donor never met what I considered his commitment.

It was during this campaign that I called another potential donor in Palm Beach, Florida, and as I was describing our organization, I mentioned that Archibald Cox, Jr., was our committee vice-chairman. The woman interrupted and asked, "Do you mean the son of *the* Archibald Cox?" When I said yes, she hung up on me. Nixon still had some supporters after Watergate.

In our final Enterprise newsletter, we quoted from Kipling's *Recessional*:

> "The tumult and the shouting dies,
> the captains and the kings depart..."

There really was an end to a syndicate's life in 1977, a sense of finality, not just postponement or prolongation.

Despite the disappointing outcome, the Enterprise years were a happy transition for me from forty-seven years on Wall Street. Eleanor and I made lasting friendships, and were faced with and met many challenges. A business was started from scratch and wound up at a profit, free from any legal problems. It was a learning bonanza. We know that our participation did help the New York Yacht Club ultimately defend the Cup successfully.

And from all of this, there were destined to be other times and other places.

CHAPTER 2

WINNING

 fter the disappointing performance of *Enterprise* in 1977, I told Fritz Jewett that I planned to resign. As manager of a losing effort to win the chance to defend the America's Cup, I felt it proper to offer my resignation. The Maritime College at Fort Schuyler Foundation had been left with substantial cash and assets, the most important of which was the 12-meter *Enterprise*.

The foundation, sensibly, agreed to keep *Enterprise*, pending a decision to be part of the next Cup campaign slated for 1980. To my pleasant surprise, Fritz Jewett asked me to remain as manager. After the 1977 effort, there was no doubt in our minds that for the next effort Dennis Conner should be the skipper, and Sparkman & Stephens the designer. Admiral Kinney and the foundation trustees agreed, subject to approval of a battle plan and budget.

The Jewetts invited Dennis and me to their summer home at Woods Hole, Massachusetts to begin formulating a battle plan. Dennis was asked what his thoughts were concerning his participation in the next Cup defense.

1. He was concerned about the treatment his wife and two daughters would receive. In 1974, they had a bad experience. As I recall, Judy and the girls had felt very much the outsiders, having been provided accommodations away from the crew house. We assured him that his family would be well cared for.

2. He would not want to be fired, except for physical/health reasons. With the bitter taste in our mouths from the firing of Lowell North, we were only too happy to agree.

3. He wanted a two-boat effort, *Enterprise* and a new 12-meter to be designed by Sparkman & Stephens, with Olin directly involved. I hesitated, thinking of the

1980

Freedom Syndicate

CHAIRMAN
G.F. Jewett, Jr.

GENERAL MANAGER
Ed du Moulin

SKIPPER
Dennis Conner

DESIGNER
Sparkman & Stephens

BUILDER
Minneford's

budget, but the Jewetts, without pause, said "go for it."

There never was a discussion of compensation with Dennis. Naturally, he would be reimbursed for any direct travel expenses relating to the campaign. In fact, the 1980 and 1983 campaigns actually cost him money by diverting his full attention from his drapery business. There was no signed agreement, nor did we ever have one during the many campaigns we worked together. Just a simple handshake.

Fritz Jewett, Dennis, and I worked as a very real "dream team" in that we shared mutual respect and trust, and our egos were not a problem. Our varied experiences were complementary.

Our initial budget was set at $1,500,000. We would, of course, have the use of *Enterprise* and other assets owned by the foundation. We managed this budget well. When the campaign was successfully concluded in 1980, the foundation was left with additional cash and assets. The foundation sold *Enterprise* for $330,000 and retained *Freedom* for the 1983 defense.

For the 1980 campaign, Dennis felt strongly that we should avoid the large research and design costs of the *Enterprise* (1977) and *Courageous* (1974) efforts – approximately $350,000 each. Olin, perhaps somewhat reluctantly, agreed. However, he did a fine job in developing our new 12-meter. The new boat was named *Freedom*, and was built in the Minneford Yard in City Island, New York, where most of the winning twelves had been constructed. With no innovative model testing, Olin Stephens and his design team at Sparkman & Stephens came up with a low freeboard design. When completed, we had a powerful boat, particularly in heavy conditions. (After 1980, a ruling came out against such low freeboard. However, *Freedom* was "grandfathered.")

On October 31, 1978, Fritz Jewett, Dennis Conner, Admiral Kinney, Steve Van Dyck, who had been the tactician on *Intrepid* when she won the Cup in 1967, and myself met with flag officers of the New York Yacht Club, and the chairman of the America's Cup Committee, Robert McCullough. It was a productive meeting, resulting in approval of our syndicate by the defending club.

The Cup Committee would have preferred that we enter both *Enterprise* and *Freedom* in the trials against *Defender* and *Courageous*. However, it was Dennis' wish to place full effort into the best boat, with the best crew. Sceptics felt that Dennis could not maintain a second team, that he would lose crew. In all the campaigns during which I worked with Dennis, and there turned out to be quite a few, this never did happen. One reason was the respect crewmembers had for Dennis. This existed even in losing efforts. Unless one has sailed with him it is difficult to appreciate how smoothly Dennis runs a boat, with minimal talk and a minimum of confusion.

Another reason for Dennis' success with his crews was Jack Sutphen, a product of the prestigious Larchmont (New York) Yacht Club. Jack's racing experience ranged from dinghies to large ocean racing yachts. He was for a long time associated with the fine old-line sailmakers, Ratsey & Lapthorn. When Dennis was invited on board *Courageous* in 1974, it was Jack who stepped aside. The ultimate team player, Jack took his replacement gracefully. After Dennis joined the 1980 campaign, he asked Jack to join the program. Jack and I discussed this, after which Jack made a big life-style change, moving, as it turned out permanently, from the East Coast to San Diego. Jack quickly became our crew "chaplain," particularly with respect to the back-up crew. He probably sailed more miles in 12-meters than anyone but Dennis, and Jack was a superb trial horse skipper.

Let me relate one example of Jack's coolness under fire: In 1974, I was sailing on *La Forza Del Destino*, a 60-foot speedster racing from Nassau to Miami. Tom Blackaller was the guest helmsman. Also on board was the famous Warwick "Commodore" Tompkins. A heavy northerly was blowing against the Gulf Stream. Rounding Great Isaac's Light in the dark, foolishly carrying a reaching spinnaker, we hit Brothers Reef. We survived, but *La Forza* sported a large gash on her keel.

Several hours after our bad experience, the yacht *Mary E* (39 feet) from Michigan in a smaller class had experienced even more severe trouble after rounding Great Isaac's. She suffered structural damage, and was sinking. It was Jack Sutphen in his 39-foot Carter who saved all nine aboard the sinking vessel, thanks to his superb seamanship in extreme conditions. There is lasting proof in that while making this rescue, Jack had a photographer from *Sports Illustrated* on his bow. Jack later presented a fascinating slide show.

Jack still sails with and against Dennis in local competition, and is often asked to sail one of Dennis' old Cup boats. He and Dennis have great respect for one another.

The staggering number of hours Dennis spends in testing sails, boats, crew, and tactics is unmatched. Even with a slow boat, you could be sure he would put up a tremendous fight, win or lose. Dennis has the ability to get people to work tirelessly with him. An example that always impressed me involves John Marshall, a brilliant, scientific, driven sailor, who was with North Sails (later president); and Tom Whidden, Dennis' perennial right hand on the racecourse. Tom is a sailmaker, too, then with rival Sobstad Sails. Currently, Whidden is president of North Sails.

North Sails had a proven reputation, and the inside track on sails for our boats. Marshall was concerned that Tom would cut into his territory. Dennis, with the greatest diplomacy and determination, encouraged Tom to develop spinnakers to be matched against North's. Pretty soon, some of our best spinnakers were made by Sobstad. Dennis was able to treat both John and Tom in a manner which each respected and, with them, develop the very best sails possible. Dennis, in his early days, had worked for a sailmaker and knew exactly what he wanted.

One of the America's Cup relationships I take great pride in was that with the Maritime College at Ft. Schuyler. Founded in 1874, the Maritime College is a well-run, low-key school, producing fine deck officers for the Navy and Merchant Marine as well as competent engineers. Its graduates are readily hired by maritime organizations. As I mentioned earlier, it was the America's Cup that led to the establishment of the foundation in 1976. The guiding hand was Admiral Sheldon Kinney. When he turned over the presidency of the College and foundation to Admiral Floyd Miller, the third Cup campaign was under way. Admiral Miller was just as enthusiastic as Admiral Kinney.

As trustee being held responsible by the foundation for the three campaigns, I was aware that a close working relationship ensured a successful experience. And it was successful. Each campaign resulted in substantial cash and assets, amounting to several million dollars. With added income generated each year, the trustees would approve programs for the benefit of the cadet corps. Funds were used for such projects as work studies, scholarships, the sailing program, gym equipment, computers, cadet comfort, and student aid. Yachts donated to the foundation were either chartered, sold, or used by the sailing team. About $1,000,000 was generated from the sales of the foundation's twelve-meters, alone. Today, the foundation is alive and well.

There were times when as many as 10 cadets participated in our America's Cup campaigns. The Maritime's training ship, *Empire State*, following its annual cruise to Europe, would rendezvous with us in Newport to give the 600 cadets on board a chance to see their Cup boats sailing, and later to meet the Cup crews.

I recall a scary moment in 1977 as the *Empire State* entered Narragansett Bay. *Enterprise* sailed out to meet the ship, past the approaching bow, only to become becalmed in the wind shadow of the 500-foot-long ship. In spite of *Enterprise*'s tall mast, she could not be seen from the bridge. After several heart-stopping moments, *Enterprise* miraculously escaped without further incident.

Thanks to the fine legal watchdogs, particularly Harman Hawkins and Ed Brady, our syndicate avoided all legal problems. They served, as we all did, without compensation. Whether we won or lost, I always felt that each campaign was a win-win situation. And for me, as manager, there was tremendous compensation in the form of the personal satisfaction that comes from starting a business from scratch, managing its growth, and liquidating it at a profit three years later.

We received aid from many areas, including that from our support vessels, particularly the tender. We were fortunate that yachtsmen of the caliber of Briggs Cunningham and, later, Arthur Wullschleger, allowed us to use their seaworthy yachts. We were responsible only for the operating expenses of these boats.

Many of our major supporters permitted us to use their yachts for race watching by our syndicate friends and families of our crews. If one were to add up all of the contributions-in-kind of this sort, they would amount to substantial dollars, and our budgets would have been far beyond what they actually were.

The actual on-the-water sailing was merely the tip of the organizational iceberg for an America's Cup campaign, but it was taken seriously. Dennis and Jack Sutphen spent record numbers of hours racing and sail-testing against each other, with both boats fully crewed and involved, over three seasons. This was in contrast to the pre-1977 days when an America's Cup campaign might total little more than a year's involvement, including a six-month sailing period.

When we first gathered in Newport in 1979, on a Friday evening, Dennis suggested the entire crew all go to the Candy Store, a favorite Newport watering hole. Jack Sutphen and I were old enough to be the fathers in this group. Dennis encouraged all of us to relax and have a drink or two. Or more... Around midnight, Jack and I gave up, and returned to the crew house. DC and the crew followed some time later.

The next morning the schedule called for an early start. Most of the younger crew members were hung over. Dennis conducted an extraordinary physical drill, sailing most of the day. Tongues were hanging out. On the boat, on the way back to base under tow, Dennis held his usual crew meeting.

He explained that he himself had "made it," but that the crew were only starting out and had to prove themselves. He had pushed them the night before at the bar, as an example of how *not* to handle themselves. The message registered. I can't recall ever having a problem with late nights or drinking from the crew.

Whereas Dennis was always relaxed on board, he was truly uptight on shore. On the dock, he walked with tunnel vision, often ignoring me, VIPs, his own crew. Necessity required that I figure out a way to get his attention. And I did. After dinner, Dennis would be exhausted from a long day on and off the water. He would wander upstairs, lie down on one of the twin beds in my room, and bitch about the frustrations of the day (media pressure, the bendy mast, the tender driver, social demands, whatever). I would make mental notes of the items that could be dealt with realistically. He would then fall asleep. Judy Conner, my wife Eleanor, and I would half-carry him to his room. The next day, I would have a good idea what to do to keep the pressure off, a manager's duty. In Dennis' book *The Art of Winning*, he describes this relationship.

Those who crewed on his boats learned a great deal. John Marshall and Tom Whidden both rose to the top of their profession, in no small part due to their association with Dennis. Three of our Maritime cadets contributed especially to our programs. Bill Trenkle went on to become Dennis' right arm as operations manager for Team Dennis Conner, and still is a key crew member. Tom Rich runs the New England Boatworks in Portsmouth, Rhode Island. He built one of Dennis' Whitbread boats, as well as his newest *Stars&Stripes*, which almost made the challenger finals in New Zealand for America's Cup 2000. A third outstanding cadet was Scott Vogel, our invaluable bow man, who is now a naval architect. His wife Dory, a seagoing ship's officer and a Maritime graduate, was a fine back-up navigator on the team.

In March of 1980, while we were still in San Diego, we had been invited to sail for the California Yacht Club's Cal Cup. As guests at the Conner home, we were discussing our plans for this regatta when Dennis mentioned he knew Bo Derek (the famous "10" movie actress). How would we like to have her join us for the Cal Cup? We were all skeptical. Dennis picked up the phone, and connected with Bo, who agreed to go sailing with the crew. *Enterprise* and *Freedom* raced against each other. Malin Burnham, on *Enterprise*, won the race. Bo was on board *Freedom* with Dennis. They lost, I'm sure, because the crew was distracted by our beautiful guest. This was one time when winning wasn't everything.

While at the California Yacht Club, I received a call from my office in New York and had to return. At that time I was chairman of my firm's Audit Committee. I learned we were in the middle of a silver crisis involving the Hunts of Texas. They almost put our 100-year-old brokerage firm out of business. This drama was being played out during the Newport trials. I frequently had to return to New York by seaplane, sometimes going from our tender directly to the plane.

Anyone who has managed a Cup campaign with its many deadlines will recognize the difficulty of being involved with any activity other that the Cup program itself.

During the summer of 1980, we often had to take care of special guests such as Vice-President Bush, and Secretary of Defense Harold Brown. This necessitated working with the Secret Service while on the water, which was an interesting experience. And on one occasion, Jackie Kennedy paid us a visit. Of all places, she wanted to eat at McDonalds. Such visitors added to the glamour for all of us.

In 1980, practically all of our funds came from individuals, not corporations. The larger donors (VIPs), both actual and potential, had to be handled with care. This wasn't always easy. I recall an eight o'clock dinner at the Clarke Cook House, planned on a race day, so a potentially large donor and his wife could meet Dennis. We waited for our guests for over an hour. Finally, we were able to contact our missing guests, who advised us that they were tired and had taken a nap. Dennis was at least as tired, after a long day at sea. They finally showed up at 10 p.m. without a word of apology. It was not a happy gathering. We excused Dennis before dessert. A small, token donation resulted from this effort. You can't win them all.

Late in the summer, we learned that the Aussies were developing a sharply curved mast which would give them added sail area without penalty. This would be of particular value in light weather conditions. We had a serious discussion whether or not we should try to duplicate it. Wisely, we decided not to do so, as we had *Freedom* well-tuned, and time was running out.

We did have a fright in the second race against *Australia*, when we lost to Jim Hardy by 28 seconds, in very light conditions.

In that race, we finished after the sun had set but just before the time limit expired. The rules specifically called for the use of running lights after sunset. Our check lists paid off. Our lights worked. However, *Australia* failed to display theirs. If they had them on board, they were probably corroded. Dennis decided to protest this violation. He felt that it should be up to the NYYC to decide if they wanted to pursue the protest; unless he filed the protest, the Club would not have that option.

Once ashore, the press went to work leading an uproar about the poor sportsmanship of such a protest. After all, how often had the challenger won a race? Dennis always represented our syndicate at the press conferences following each race. In this instance, the Cup Committee "invited" him to discuss the protest with them. Dennis asked me to cover for him at the press conference. This caused more criticism against Dennis. The press accused him of being afraid to face them.

After dinner, Dennis, John Marshall, Steve Van Dyck, Fritz Jewett, and I met. Marshall, always tough, urged following through with the protest. The majority agreed. As manager, I wanted to drop it, and felt strongly enough to offer my resignation if the protest was pursued.

Meanwhile, the Cup Committee was at Stan Livingston's home in Bristol, trying to resolve the problem. At one in the morning, it appeared they would proceed with the protest. Our group turned in, and would reconvene at 0600. I invited Jack Sutphen and Halsey Herreshoff to join our morning meeting. I needed some backing, and was confident that they would support my view. They did. At this point, the phone rang. We were informed that the Cup Committee agreed to withdraw the protest, although not unanimously.

But when the Cup Committee tried to do so, they were informed that it could not be withdrawn. Cleverly, the Protest Committee then disallowed the protest on the basis that we had in fact made a typographical error in filling out the protest form. Another international crisis averted.

The 1980 trials were not as exciting as 1974 and 1977. The competition was just not as intense. Ted Turner, with the venerable *Courageous*, had his mind elsewhere. Tom Blackaller added dash to the summer, sailing *Defender* with Russell Long. Tom was every bit as colorful as Ted. He was outstandingly handsome and flamboyant. A two-time Star World Champion, Tom sailed against Dennis over many years, and was a fierce competitor on the water. When Tom died about eleven years ago, the sailing world suffered a great loss.

It was a memorable day when we eliminated *Australia*. Dennis invited her skipper Jim Hardy to sail *Freedom* into Newport Harbor. Many of us, including Eleanor, transferred by rubber boat from our tender to *Freedom* for the victory sail into Newport on this dreary gray day. Little did we know that this would be the last successful New York Yacht Club defense of the millennium, and beyond.

The Australian's bendy mast showed that to win, the challenger has to take design chances that the defender might be reluctant to do. If ever you look at the half models of the 12-meters in the Model Room of the New York Yacht Club, with the exception of *Intrepid*, there is little variation. The challenger sought new horizons. This philosophy paid off in 1983, with the innovative winged keel.

In 1980, our final budget was $2,000,000. *Freedom*, cash, and much equipment remained with the foundation. We were all still speaking to each other, and we were ready for the next – and fateful – defense. Dennis was sure we would lose the Cup one day. He only hoped he would not be that skipper. I sure hoped that I would not be that syndicate's manager.

Freedom, which did such a wonderful job in 1980, was retained by the foundation as a bench mark and trial horse for a possible defense in 1983. But in planning for his next effort, Dennis boldly dreamt of two or three *new* designs. What Dennis wants he usually gets.

CHAPTER 3

LOSING

n April 10, 1981, the Board of Trustees of the Maritime College at Ft. Schuyler Foundation formally approved a proposal from George F. Jewett, Jr. to defend the America's Cup for the third time. Rear Admiral Floyd Miller, who was to replace Rear Admiral Kinney as president of the College, came aboard in 1982. He and Admiral Kinney worked hand in hand to support the America's Cup program. After our decisive win in 1980 and the excellent condition of the foundation, it was not too difficult to marshal its support, that of the New York Yacht Club, and of our major backers for a new defense effort.

I would continue as the trustee responsible for the program. Fritz Jewett would stand as chairman and, of course, Dennis Conner as skipper. We would continue to work as a closely knit team.

With *Freedom* as the benchmark, our syndicate planned to build two new boats and retain two different designers: Sparkman & Stephens (S&S) would design one and Johan Valentijn, the other. We were looking back in time to when a combination of two designers had worked remarkably well; that is, when Olin Stephens, Jr. collaborated with W. Starling Burgess to design *Ranger* for the 1937 defense.

In the 1980's, Olin Stephens was semi-retired from S&S. Young Bill Langan would be the S&S designer. Johan, while born Dutch, was a citizen of the U.S., qualifying him to design an American contender. He had considerable experience having worked for S&S. He had co-designed *Australia* with Ben Lexcen, and designed *France III* for Baron Bich.

We hoped that one of the two new designs, after careful testing, would produce a boat superior to *Freedom*. But it soon became apparent that neither of the

1983

LIBERTY SYNDICATE

CHAIRMAN
G.F. Jewett, Jr.

GENERAL MANAGER
Ed du Moulin

SKIPPER
Dennis Conner

DESIGNER
J. Valentijn

BUILDER
Newport Offshore

two new boats – *Magic* (designed by Valentijn) nor *Spirit of America* (S&S designed) – would give us the edge we desired. With the experience gained from this unprecedented program, we decided to go for a third boat. Although there was rumor that we actually planned to use *Freedom*, or that we should do so, that never was our intention.

Before proceeding with a third boat, we had to convince the foundation, the New York Yacht Club and our major backers to support this addition to our program. With our good record of working within and maintaining tight control over

our budget, originally set at $4,000,000, we received approval to go ahead. We were confident that the extra funds would be forthcoming, and that we would meet our financial obligations to the foundation. All of these goals were, in fact, met.

Before considering a third boat, we allocated $100,000 to give Bill Langan (S&S) the opportunity to make design changes to *Spirit of America*. Unfortunately, these changes did not produce any significant improvement.

We had hoped that Bill Langan and Johan Valentijn would be able to work together, freely reviewing each others plans, and eventually coming up, through collaboration, with a winner. This cooperation did not develop, forcing us to select one or the other. It was an agoniz-

AUSTRALIA II

ing experience.

During this period, Olin and I, with the help of Halsey Herreshoff, did our best to make the cooperative effort work. Our committee was convinced that we had to go with Johan. Bill Langan, who was also trying to manage S&S, could not devote full time to our project. On the other hand, Johan, who lived in Newport, could give us his full time and energy.

When the news of our selection became public there was an outcry, primarily from old-line members of the NYYC, that we had mistreated Olin Stephens and S&S. During this whole process Halsey Herreshoff was closely involved. He recognized the issues and often discussed them with Olin. I would refer the critics to Halsey who was considered by everyone to be a person of the highest integrity. I would emphasize that Fritz Jewett, Dennis Conner, and I, to this day, have the greatest respect for Olin Stephens. And we had it then, but Olin was not running the S&S show.

The collaborative process would work again, when Malin Burnham and Dennis Conner would organize the San Diego Yacht Club's challenge to bring the Cup back from Australia in 1987. For that campaign, they put together a very talented team of designers: Britton Chance, Bruce Nelson, and Dave Pedrick worked together, under John Marshall's leadership.

Our new Valentijn-designed 12-meter named *Liberty* was built in Newport and trucked to San Diego where she was christened, and then launched at the Driscoll Shipyard.

With 1974's sad and frustrating memory of the red-hulled *Mariner* still clear in her mind, my wife Eleanor mentioned that she was not happy with the choice of the color red for *Liberty*'s hull. However, the boat proved fast enough to eliminate the other contenders – John Kolius on *Courageous* and Tom Blackaller on *Defender*. *Liberty* was a demonstrably fast 12-meter, particularly in 15-to-18 knots of wind – probably the fastest "conventional" one of her class.

After our hard-earned selection by the America's Cup Committee to be the defender against *Australia II*, as was customary, the Courageous/Defender syndicate offered us the use of sails and equipment after they had been excused from competition. The tradition of selection by the famous "straw hats" would disappear after this Cup, and be replaced by a selection based purely on a point system. But in 1983, selection was still the manner in which defenders were chosen.

Let me digress just a bit here to say that I feel the New York Yacht Club never fully appreciated Dennis' tremendous performance on their behalf in the 1983 *Liberty* campaign. To my mind, and to others who know him well, Dennis' team leadership abilities combined with his growing understanding of the cooperation between sailing and sponsorship, and his ability to live within a prescribed budget, far outweighed some of his social shortcomings. If a partnership between Dennis and the NYYC had been established, I was confident that the Maritime Foundation would have participated in another campaign. And in that case, *Liberty*, and other assets, might have been at the disposal of the NYYC.

As it happened, when Dennis decided to mount a challenge on behalf of the San Diego Yacht Club, the foundation had concerns. The SDYC would be 3,000 miles away; the defense halfway around the world, and the budget would be substantially more than in prior campaigns.

After the 1983 campaign, there were at least three organizations interested in buying *Liberty*, her sails and equipment. Since I was also part of Dennis Conner's group, I excused myself from the decision-making of the trustees. I was happy to learn that Dennis was the successful bidder. After all, Dennis contributed greatly to the foundation, at a personal sacrifice, and deserved to acquire the assets. His bid was the highest received. But I get ahead of myself. Such is the lucky nature of my association with the America's Cup that one campaign necessarily becomes interwoven with the past and the future.

Let's return to the battlefield. Our syndicate had a difficult time in 1983. The summer was dominated by the controversial keel on *Australia II*. Much of Dennis' and my time was taken up with meetings with members of the Cup Committee discussing our options for what came to be known as "Keelgate." It all started to come to light in June of 1983, when *Liberty*'s navigator Halsey Herreshoff sketched what he thought the Aussie keel looked like. He openly argued that *Australia II* was a 12-and a-*half* meter and that, if no adjustment were made, we would lose the Cup.

We were also convinced that the Dutch were the real designers of the winged keel. The Cup Committee had substantial evidence that this was so, but was unable to obtain written affirmation of the verbal statements related to a NYYC representative when he visited Holland to question the Dutch designers. The rules require that Cup boats be designed by nationals of their respective countries. We had been told this rule had been broken by the Australians, but we had no written proof.

Australia II had an outstanding record in winning the challenger trials. She had ably demonstrated her quickness, and her downwind speed seemed good. When we went head to head with her, Dennis avoided close circling starting maneuvers and tacking duels, because *Australia II* could turn on a dime and out-accelerate any boat on the water. He depended primarily on wind shifts. *Australia II*'s downwind speed against us proved to be nothing short of awesome, leading some of us to believe that she had been "sandbagging" in the challenger series. It was *Australia II*'s ability to fly before the wind that led to our dramatic, traumatic defeat.

Once again, I have jumped ahead of my story.

Warren Jones was Alan Bond's righthand man. I had to admire his tenacity and his ability to use the American press in a most effective way. It was my impression that Bond/Jones set a precedent in their determination to use the press to demoralize the opposition (us). It certainly didn't make life any easier. Of course, this defense created much greater public interest as the drama unfolded, on land and on the water. I must admit I admired Jones gamesmanship and manipulative powers. We were no match for him.

Our syndicate decided that a cablegram should be sent to the Netherlands Ship Model Basin, offering to buy the keel plans. I was asked to sign it as the manager. Very reluctantly, I did so. Alan Bond got his hands on the cablegram and, with Warren's help, made the most of it. There never was any intention on the part of our syndicate to use such plans, even if we had obtained them. That was not why we were trying to obtain them. But Warren Jones very effectively created a great deal of publicity at my expense. Ours was a näive effort to smoke them out, an ill-conceived attempt to prove that the Dutch controlled the design.

The Australian keel dramatics continued right up to the start of the actual America's Cup races. On September 12, just hours before the "captains' meeting" (a briefing conducted by the America's Cup Committee with representatives of the challenger and defender), the Cup Committee was considering canceling the Cup racing. The late America's Cup Hall-of-Famer, Victor Romagna, secretary of the Cup Committee, strongly believed *Australia II* had been designed outside the rules, and should be disqualified. But by a 5 to 4 vote, it was decided to proceed with the defense. It is difficult to imagine what might have happened if the vote had gone the other way. Certainly, the America's Cup would have wound up in the New York courts, as would occur four years later – for a different reason.

On the racecourse, *Liberty*, to our surprise and delight, had built up an astonishing record in the finals. With the score 3 to 1 in our favor, a rare breakdown gave the Aussies a window of opportunity.

It was a windy day (18 knots) with a choppy sea, conditions that favored us. About forty-five minutes before the start, as *Liberty* was tuning up, the port jumper piston tensioner broke. Dennis headed downwind as slowly as possible, to avoid getting too far from the starting area, and sent our two best men up the mast, Maritime College graduates Tom Rich and Scott Vogel. They were tossed around like men on a flying trapeze.

We were informed that the replacement part was ashore. I tried to get the

Coast Guard helicopter to run it out to us, without success. We sent our fastest chase boat *Rhonda* to our Newport base. Back out she sped. Tom and Scott were still aloft, still bouncing and swaying back and forth. But alas, the spare part did not fit.

In all our campaigns, I can't recall such a problem as this. Desperately, Tom and Scott patched the repair, with the knowledge that it couldn't last. Down they came, bruised and exhausted. The impetus of Murphy's Law was taking over. The jib had been damaged while hoisting it downwind. The crew replaced it in minutes. We finally squared away – *after* the warning gun.

But Dennis rose to the occasion. He calmly won the start by 37 seconds. On the first leg the make-do repair let go as expected. We lost the race by one minute 47 seconds. The score was narrowing, now 3 to 2 in *Liberty*'s favor.

Race 6 was a disaster, but not from any rigging failure. The wind was about 15 knots from the northwest. Again, not a bad breeze for *Liberty*. Halsey Herreshoff, our navigator, was very familiar with northwesterlies. But *Australia II* sailed into a tremendous and rare wind shift, a breeze of her own. We lost by the staggering time of three minutes 25 seconds. Score 3 to 3. And now, what was referred to as the "race of the century" was at hand.

The seventh and deciding race remains one of the most exciting of my Cup experiences. After *Liberty* rounded the fourth mark with a 57-second lead, I glanced over to the Australia tender, and noticed a quiet Alan Bond. I am admittedly nervous, no matter how big our lead. I left the bridge of *Fire 3*, our tender, and met with Jack Sutphen and my son Richard, both afterguard veterans. Much to my astonishment, they said we would likely lose this downwind leg. I could not believe it. They explained that on the second reaching leg, the wind had shifted, and the leg had gone from a reach to a run. On the first reaching leg, we had gained 16 seconds. On the second reaching (now *downwind*) leg, we *lost* 22 seconds. Reaching legs are shorter than the upwind/downwind legs. With wind conditions as they were, Jack and Richard believed, on this final full downwind leg, *Australia II* would pass *Liberty*.

Navigator Herreshoff was using his stadimeter (a sextant-like instrument) connected to our onboard computer to calculate the rate of change between *Liberty* and *Australia II*. The results confirmed the obvious: if *Liberty* continued on the same course, she would be passed before the downwind mark was reached. There was no panic, no fighting among the crew as some said later. Dennis was as usual cool, calm, and had everyone's full support. To avoid what appeared to be inevitable, *Liberty* executed a number of jibes to each one of *Australia II*'s. At one point, the red boat was still somewhat ahead and running parallel to *Australia II*.

But sailing lower and faster, the Aussies passed *Liberty*. This was a spectacular exhibition of her downwind speed. We trailed by 21 seconds at the bottom mark. Dennis believed, until the very end, that he could win. He and the crew never gave up.

In spite of about 50 tacks, including fake ones, and Dennis' attempts to draw her into the spectator fleet, *Australia II* won Race 7 and the America's Cup. As I once again looked across at Alan Bond, he was ecstatic as he should have been. I was calm on the outside, but had a sick feeling in the pit of my stomach – just as if I'd suffered a kangaroo kick.

The press, second-guessing sailors and other pundits, had all kinds of comments, mostly negative: too much time lost jibing; no rational excuse to lose the lead; fighting on board; poor tactics... But for having competed so closely against the ultimately worthy opponent – *Australia II*, a 12-meter of a truly revolutionary design, with its own very capable crew – our own crew and afterguard, unmatched in experience and dedication, deserved thanks and respect, not this negative carping.

t was an unprecedented series, having gone to the full seven races, and a sad, but I have to say a very proud, moment for me. Truly a turning point in America's Cup history, and I was a part of it. Our effort had been one hundred percent. There is no shame in having been beaten by a better effort. *Liberty* had sailed as hard as possible against a formidable challenger. There is no doubt that Australia's victory was the yachting community's equivalent of "the shot heard round the world."

Much of the return to the harbor was in darkness. Our tender blared out *Stars & Stripes Forever*, which was drowned out by *Waltzing Matilda* and the horns of the victors. September 26, 1983, will be etched in my mind as long as I live.

The ensuing press conference was a nightmare. Dennis handled himself well but was obviously under a heavy strain. The Newport streets overflowed with people. Traffic was at a standstill. Pandemonium was the order of the night.

President Reagan called to congratulate us on our defense. Dennis answered the call, and had a warm conversation with the president. Letters and telegrams came from all over the world, congratulating Dennis and his team for putting up such a valiant battle. But, to the victors go the spoils. The night of our loss, the crew gathered at Seaview Terrace. It was a somber affair, more like a wake. We did manage, finally, to drink the champagne we had set aside each day for the victory celebration. I don't believe any flag officer of the New York Yacht Club or any of the America's Cup Committee dropped by. The NYYC showed little appreciation for the tremendous effort made by Dennis and his crew.

In the event that the New York Yacht Club lost the Cup, plans had been made to present it to Alan Bond and the Royal Perth Yacht Club in the New York City clubhouse later in the week. At the last minute the plans were changed. Under tight security "The Old Mug" arrived in Newport at around two a.m. the next morning. It had been decided that it made logistical sense to make the presentation in Newport, where a larger crowd could be accommodated than could be handled in the 44th Street clubhouse.

That afternoon, the official ceremony took place on the veranda of the Marble House, the beautiful Harold Vanderbilt mansion, and quite appropriate for the occasion. The crew of *Australia II* was on the veranda, but our crew had not been invited to participate. Bus Mosbacher had phoned me late the previous evening, asking that I be there. To my knowledge, there was no invitation extended to any member of the *Liberty* crew, including Dennis, to attend. The Conner family had reservations the day of the ceremony to fly back to San Diego via Providence and New York, and they were on the way to the airport with dozens of suitcases. Others of the crew already were headed for home. I had spoken to the Jewetts, who were quite upset about the outcome and probably also about the lack of support from the NYYC. They would not go to the presentation. I felt that someone should represent our syndicate. Later, I learned that our navigator Halsey Herreshoff had been prevented from joining the veranda ceremony by NYYC officials. He was told he could watch it from the lawn. The only excuse I could imagine for this sort of dismissive behavior must have been complete shock at having lost.

With few words, I presented our syndicate flag to the winning skipper John Bertrand. Then Commodore Robert Stone did a fine job as he presented the Cup to the beaming Australians in a charming, relaxed, and humorous manner.

If the Cup had to be lost, many Americans were pleased to have the Aussies win it.

The evening before the Newport ceremony, I received another call from the White House. President Reagan planned to welcome the Australian crew the day after the Marble House ceremony, but in sharp contrast to the Newport ceremony, he insisted the American crew be there too. The crew was already dispersing: Bob Campbell was on his way to Boston; Tom Whidden to Essex; Dennis to San Diego, and Halsey Herreshoff was to leave for Europe the next afternoon. Through the night, I contacted the majority of our sailors. Not an easy task. But they liked the idea of a White House welcome. A team flight was booked for the next afternoon from Providence. Other than Dennis and Halsey, all of the crew were on the plane. Fritz and Lucy Jewett, Eleanor and I, were proud to be part of the entourage. Every courtesy was shown us en route to Washington. As we approached the Washington airport, the pilot informed us that the plane carrying the Aussies was arriving at the same time. However, Flight Control wanted us to beat the Australians into the Washington Airport which, of course, we did. Commodore Stone joined us at the White House.

In Washington, we received royal treatment – limousines at the airport, police escorts, guests of a local restaurant – and finally we were off to the White House. We were given a special tour. On the White House lawn, President Reagan and Vice-President Bush met both teams. The president shook everyone's hand and said encouraging words. He admired the fight we put up. Our chairman, Fritz Jewett, presented the president with mementos of the campaign. Weeks later, each of us received individually signed photographs showing the president shaking our hands. The ceremony certainly helped to restore our spirits.

Back in Newport for the cleanup, John "Chink" Longely, Bond's crew boss, visited me in our trailer office. He wanted to know how the foundation operated. Before answering, I asked him: "Where in the hell is Fremantle?" He said: "If you drilled a hole through the center of the earth, from here in Newport, you would come out in Fremantle." It took about six weeks to close our Newport operation and settle all accounts. The final budget came in under $5,000,000. The foundation ended up with more cash, with *Liberty*, and with other assets. *Freedom* was sold for $420,000 by the foundation. *Magic* was sold in Newport. *Liberty* was retained, as was *Spirit Of America*.

The following year, Admiral Sheldon Kinney retired. He had been a great support for all of us and, certainly, an effective leader in our three campaigns.

I had the dubious distinction of being the last manager of a successful defense in 1980 and the first manager to lose the Cup for the New York Yacht Club in 1983. Despite the rumors, Dennis Conner's head was not put on display in the glass case inside the club where the Cup had rested for so many decades. But from this agonizing defeat, Dennis, like the phoenix, would rise from the ashes to return the Cup to our shores. Only this time, the Cup would be in the custody of the San Diego Yacht Club. No one could visualize the revolution, the upheaval, that would follow. Through controversy, catamarans, and courts, the America's Cup would live on.

It took me several months to close our Newport headquarters, break down out shipyard, store and insure our equipment for future use, and make an accurate inventory of everything we had on hand. Then there was office work, the job of making appropriate thank-yous to so many who had helped us along the way, and have final goodbyes with close associates in Newport.

One interesting sidelight: John Storck, Jr., had donated an American Motors Eagle as our official syndicate car for use in Newport. I arranged to purchase the car from the foundation, and my grandson, Edward du Moulin, now proudly drives it to and from school in Larchmont, New York, almost two decades later.

While terminating our operation in all these ways, not a day passed that I couldn't still hear the cheers and feel the tears of a hard-fought campaign.

CHAPTER 4

COMEBACK

The moment *Australia II* crossed the finish line in 1983, ending the longest winning streak in sports history, a new era was ushered in. The America's Cup could never be the same.

Shortly after the loss of the Cup, serious plans were being made to "get the Cup back." There were a great many behind-the-scenes meetings. Both Dennis Conner, who was to be commodore of the San Diego Yacht Club in 1984, and the New York Yacht Club were interested in working through the Maritime College Foundation. I was anxious to help put together the effort to return the Cup to the U.S.A. Several months after we lost the Cup, I met with Commodore Robert Stone of the NYYC and suggested that Dennis be invited to represent the club in such a quest. Since he had lost the Cup, I knew that Dennis wanted to give the NYYC first call on his services.

Although I would not manage a new effort, I was willing to help in the background. The Maritime Foundation owned *Liberty* and its equipment, and likely would be interested. The Foundation already had received offers to purchase *Liberty* from various groups. My idea was to ask John Kolius, nine years younger than Dennis, to be backup skipper and to sail the second boat. Kolius, after *Courageous* was eliminated in 1983, had graciously practiced against Dennis and they got along very well. The plan would be that after "winning back the Cup" Dennis would turn over the helm to John (as he later did in 1995 with Paul Cayard, and in 2000 with young Ken Read). Commodore Stone said that he liked the idea. Several days later, he advised that Kolius wanted to head his own program for the NYYC. Kolius missed an opportunity to learn from the master. Dennis did not learn about this proposal until many years later.

48

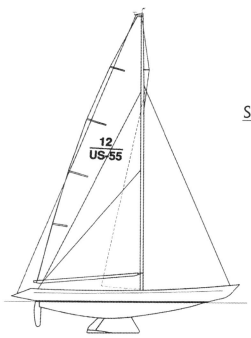

1987

STARS & STRIPES SYNDICATE

CHAIRMAN / MANAGER
Malin Burnham

EXECUTIVE DIRECTOR
H. P. Purdon

SKIPPER
Dennis Conner

DESIGN TEAM COORDINATOR
John Marshall

DESIGN TEAM
Britton Chance,
Bruce Nelson,
David Pedrick

BUILDER
Bob Derecktor

In December, 1984, Eleanor and I were in Spokane, Washington, to attend the wedding of Betsy Jewett. It was a gala affair as only the Jewetts could do it. Dennis buttonholed me in the checkroom. He asked me to read a short concise plan to win back the Cup. It called for an astonishing budget of $15,000,000. I was glad that I would not be manager. It was a formidable amount of money, but I had no doubt Dennis could raise such a sum, and I would help.

With 14 international challengers seeking the Cup, the NYYC had no assurance that the Cup would return to its former pedestal at the 44th Street clubhouse in New York. Although Dennis Conner would have preferred to represent the NYYC, efforts to get together failed. Our 1980/1983 entente was not to continue.

Dennis became impatient waiting for a decision from the NYYC. Many rumors circulated about skipper selection, and these did nothing to help calm Dennis' impatience. Finally, Dennis received a call from Commodore Emil Mosbacher's secretary, *ordering* him to be at the New York Yacht Club for a meeting on the approaching Friday evening, the very night that Dennis was being honored, across the continent, by the San Diego Yacht Club on becoming commodore. For Dennis, becoming commodore was a dream come true. He tried to change the date of the NYYC's meeting to no avail. Frustrated by the yacht club's seeming indifference, he decided that he would be unable to work comfortably in this command performance atmosphere. Fritz Jewett, Malin Burnham, and I asked him to remain calm until we were able to contact Commodores Stone and Mosbacher and advise them of Dennis' decision. Over that weekend, we contacted them both, advising that a public announcement would be issued on the following Wednesday. This would give the NYYC ample opportunity to prepare their own announcement. Our press release appeared as planned. The NYYC release came later that week. John Kolius, skipper of *Courageous* in 1983, would be skipper of their challenger. He brought with him the financial backing of several influential fellow Texans. Sparkman & Stephens would be their designer, with young William Langan in charge.

Dennis, with the moral and financial support of his longtime close friend Malin Burnham, decided to form a syndicate on behalf of the San Diego Yacht Club. At that time Admiral Kinney received a petition signed by 300 cadets urging the Maritime College Foundation to participate in the challenge to regain the Cup. It was a great testimonial to our past relations and the benefits the College and cadets had received.

Both Dennis and the NYYC approached the Maritime Foundation with the hope that it would be part of the challenge. But the size of the budget and the distance to Fremantle, halfway around the world, were not risks the foundation wanted to take. Perhaps if Dennis and the Jewetts had been part of the NYYC's program, Maritime would have participated.

Malin Burnham, a former Star World Champion, member of the *Enterprise* afterguard in 1977 and an outstanding business leader in San Diego, helped establish the Sail America Foundation for International Understanding. He would be chairman. I agreed to serve as a trustee for a period of one year to help the program get off the ground. Fritz Jewett and John Marshall were elected to the board, as was Dennis. My reason for serving for only one year was primarily based on my living 3,000 miles away. I was honored to later become emeritus. I would continue to help as an advisor to Malin and Dennis.

Sir Thomas Lipton benefited commercially from his many unsuccessful challenges, as did Baron Marcel Bich, but their prime interest was to capture "The Old Mug." Basically, they were sportsmen. The 1987 Australian defense would change, forever, those good old days. To raise the money to fund the '87 challenges would require substantial corporate contributions. Skippers and most of the crews would be compensated. It was somewhat of a return to the days before the 12-meter era when crews were strictly professionals. In those times, there was a strong social difference between the afterguard and the professional crews (many of whom were Scandinavians). With the advent of the 12s in 1958, the crews were considered family.

Corporations had to justify their investments, thus the rules were changed to permit advertising onboard the Cup boats. Corporations demanded attention from the skippers which impinged on their time and energy. Dennis was particularly affected, since he devoted what I felt was much too much time entertaining and giving talks to corporate staff. However, Dennis' close relations with the companies assured their continued support. A well-known sports writer told me that Dennis gave more of himself to his corporate sponsors than any sports figure he knew.

To help bridge the gap between our old organization and that of Sail America, I suggested they retain Joanne Fishman, yachting correspondent for the *New York Times*, with a broad knowledge of the Cup. She became project coordinator and, in the important initial stages, was effective. Unable to relocate to California, she found it difficult to "coordinate" from 3,000 miles away and the relationship ended.

The day-to-day responsibilities rested with H.P. "Sandy" Purdon, veteran sailor and San Diego businessman. He became executive administrator.

John Marshall was responsible for the design team. He was outstanding in this role. John, with a background as a scientist/engineer; sailing experience that included four America's Cup campaigns; and excellent leadership qualities, deserves a large share of the credit for our ultimate victory.

Science Applications International, (SAIC), a major high-tech contractor for the U.S. Department of Defense, agreed to work closely with our design team. Malin was fortunate in having J. Robert Beyster, president of SAIC on his board. Marshall and Beyster were an effective team in applying American space age technology to yacht design.

Michael Dingman was introduced to the Cup scene by Malin. He was then, and is now, one of the most successful corporate leaders in America. As then-head of The Henley Group, a major U.S. corporation, he opened many corporate doors for Malin and Dennis. Most of our major sponsors came to us in this manner. Dennis was, and is, the best corporate fund raiser on the America's Cup scene. Once the event went commercial, following other sports such as golf and tennis, budgets grew and television became the means to make the public aware. Competing for the America's Cup would no longer be strictly one country's organized yacht club against another country's. It would become a major world sporting event steeped in commercialism. Perhaps this is progress. I don't think so.

The introduction of onboard cameras and microphones by ESPN, and Gary Jobson's knowledgeable commentary made it an exciting, more understandable spectator sport. In my opinion, the scene in Fremantle will never be duplicated. The facilities may be topped, but the fantastic winds and colorful heavy seas, the hospitality of the Aussies, the intensity of the trials, the drama, all added up to a lifetime highlight.

Each day, leaving and entering the harbor, thousands would gather on the rock jetties screaming and holding amusing signs like WELL DONE DENNIS – YOU BASTARD. It wasn't unusual for a speedboat with bare-breasted girls to come as close alongside *Stars & Stripes* as possible. My binoculars were always close by my usual position on the bridge of *Betsy*. One of our most welcome VIPs on board our tender was Jimmy Buffett. He was a great morale booster, and was the featured entertainer at the lavish America's Cup Ball in Fremantle. Steve Vaus had produced our first fight song: "What Goes Down Must Come Up," as well as our "Stars & Stripes Anthem." Playing either of these songs can easily bring a tear or two to my eyes. Perhaps they should be revised for the 2003 challenge.

As the trials entered their final stages, and the Cup races began, the excitement was unbelievable. It was difficult to enter or leave our compound. At one point, Dennis received a death threat requiring that he wear a special bullet-proof vest and be accompanied by a personal bodyguard. That was the one and only negative incident.

In the "land down under," everyone seemed involved. Sailing truly is a national sport there. It can be said that the Cup was under American wraps for 132 years before Australia opened it to the world.

A major decision was made by the *Stars & Stripes* leadership: the team would not go to Fremantle in the early stages. It would even miss the 1986 World 12-Meter Championship. This raised many an eyebrow and drew much criticism from the press and major backers. Instead, an excellent compound was set up in Honolulu's Snug Harbor. *Liberty*, our important benchmark, along with a redesigned *Spirit of America*, followed by two new boats, were shipped to Hawaii. There were so many changes made that I gave up trying to identify which boat was which. You can be sure Dennis knew.

As the criticism mounted, and after receiving a call from Fritz and Lucy Jewett, I phoned Dennis in Hawaii. He didn't want to discuss it over the phone and suggested I come out and see for myself. Eleanor and I were off to see Pearl Harbor and the *Stars & Stripes* team in action. Arriving at the airport, we were met by Dot Chesebrough with orders for me to take the rubber chase boat to meet Dennis on the water. Although tired, with little sleep from the trip, I followed orders. Dick Chesebrough was waiting for me and, in a short while, I climbed aboard the 12-meter. Hand shakes all around. Among the crew was Olympic gold medal winner Robbie Haines. I was tossed some suitable seagoing gear. Off we went, testing light weather sails and boat performance. The weather and calm sea were like Long Island Sound on a summer afternoon. Lunchtime, I ate a soggy sandwich and asked for a Coke, only to be summarily corrected. I was given a Pepsi (one of

Dennis' major sponsors). Later, I made up for the slight by buying PepsiCo stock.

While eating lunch, we proceeded toward Diamond Head. I had a chance to steer a 12 (I was not sure which one) with a winged keel for the first time. In less than an hour, we were off Diamond Head. Winds of 25 knots and large seas greeted us. For hours, heavy weather sails were tested. Dennis pointed out that the early trials in Fremantle would mainly be in light weather, but the final trials, and the Cup itself, would be sailed in heavy weather conditions. While our competition was sailing in light winds, on any given day *Stars & Stripes* was doing that *and* sailing in heavy weather. Dennis and the crews would not be distracted, as they would have been in Fremantle, by the press. The spying was minimal. However, before our lunch break, a helicopter flew overhead. Dennis said that he had been alerted by "friends" at the airport that the helicopter had been commissioned to fly a "spy" over to see what Dennis was up to. At this point, Dennis moved the trim tab, changed the set of the sails. The "spy" could not have learned very much. It was also pointed out that here in Hawaii, it was far less costly for the crew to travel to and from the mainland.

A few phone calls to our concerned backers put their minds at ease. This was Dennis at his best.

Sail America was fortunate to receive a donation of a 64-foot, 44-ton Swath ship which had been designed for the U.S. Navy. With double pontoons it was a very stable vessel particularly suited for Indian Ocean waters. It was named *Betsy* (after Betsy Ross, not Betsy Jewett as many thought). By filling a pontoon with water, it would lower one side to accommodate the freeboard of a 12-meter. Years later, *Betsy* was sold for a substantial sum.

Malin and Dennis led the drive to raise the necessary funds. I worked hard soliciting our former supporters from 1977-80-83, most of whom remained loyal. This was the first time corporate contributions became the prime source of funds. Prior to this America's Cup event, personal contributions amounted to about 90 percent of the total raised. The percentages would reverse. Participation would become 90 percent corporate.

The 12s were not permitted to fly spinnakers with corporate logos while racing. Dennis would display the logos right after the finish gun. Ford was one of our major sponsors. Edsel Ford really took a personal interest and was a pleasure to work with. One afternoon, *Stars & Stripes* was displaying a Merrill Lynch spinnaker when Edsel came aboard *Betsy*. We quickly sent the Ford spinnaker to *Stars & Stripes* where a fast sail change was made. We were learning about "sponsor fulfillment."

Anyone fortunate enough to visit the Model Room of the New York Yacht Club will note the plaques accompanying the defender/challenger models. For the first time, corporations appeared on the plaque of *Stars & Stripes* (US 55). The likes of the Vanderbilts and the Morgans of the past must be frowning from above.

In 1983, we had failed to create a viable cooperative design effort. But in 1987 under John Marshall, three designers (Chance, Nelson, Pedrick) came up with a real winner for the San Diego Yacht Club. As I have noted, the New York Yacht Club had retained designer Bill Langan. At one point, a group of its members wanted to bring in another designer to work with Sparkman & Stephens. This created a crisis settled by remaining exclusively with Sparkman & Stephens. This decision may well have contributed to their early elimination.

The decision to prepare in Hawaii was one factor in the victory of *Stars & Stripes*. The determination of the design team resulting in the never-ending improvement of US 55 was a wonder to behold. One of the interesting projects was the collaboration with 3M on the "riblets" placed on the hull beneath the waterline. I am not sure they were of any great practical help, but as a psychological ploy, they were of benefit. The application of riblets was not new to our Navy's submarines.

 ennis and the crew carried the burden on the water. The competition was keen and the pressure great. Tom Blackaller with his unique *USA 1* and strong personality gave Dennis a difficult time. Dennis avoided "p---ing" contests with Tom who was loud, articulate and had a very strong vocabulary. Of course it bothered Dennis, but on board *Stars & Stripes*, all was kept calm. *USA 1*, representing the St. Francis (Y.C.) Golden Gate Challenge, was a radical design. Perhaps with more time to become familiar with her, Tom might have come out on top. She sported a bow rudder, in addition to the standard keel and stern rudder.

The spectacular success of Chris Dickson on his two fiberglass boats, aptly referred to as "Plastic Fantastics," was a considerable threat. They were the first Cup boats to be made of fiberglass. Eventually three were built. The first two were identical. Michael Fay was the leader of this challenge from New Zealand. During the trials Dickson put together an astonishing record – the best of all the challengers.

"Glassgate" was the new controversy. My wife and I visited Sydney on the way to Fremantle. The papers were full of an accusation, attributed to Dennis Conner, to the effect that New Zealand was cheating. Why else, Dennis had asked, would they build a fiberglass hull? On the way to the Sydney airport, our initially genial taxi driver asked if we were going to the America's Cup, and with whom we were involved. Proudly, I said *Stars & Stripes*. What a blast resounded from the front of the cab. The cabbie was quite upset. I was sorry to hear of another *cause célèbre*. "Keelgate" had been enough.

On the water, Dennis eliminated his adversaries one by one. With his boat primarily designed to handle the heavy seas and strong winds off Fremantle expected during the Cup, Dennis still managed to survive the light weather trials of October and November 1986 in the Indian Ocean. It was touch and go at times.

One particularly impressive race against *NZ 7* stands out in my mind. *Stars & Stripes* was leading when the genoa split. There was little commotion and little talk as the crew replaced the tattered sail with a new one. With only the mainsail, Dennis prevented *NZ 7* from passing *Stars & Stripes*. ESPN showed the world this dramatic footage.

Although Malin Burnham had asked if I could move to Fremantle in August of 1986 when the team and equipment were to arrive, I could not do so. I would be there by early December. Bill Trenkle, Dennis' operations manager and right hand, along with others, did a first class job in establishing the base of operations, after two years of planning.

Thanks to Mike Dingman, we had the use of the 135-foot *Carmac VI* for our wives, friends, and VIP's. Team banners were boldly displayed, with the cheering squad dressed in appropriate red, white and blue.

The Japanese and Alan Bond had two mega yachts that were sister ships, over 225-feet long and built in Japan, among a totally breathtaking fleet of spectator boats from all over the world including the large, later-to-become-infamous cruise ship, *Achille Lauro*. Alan Bond invited a group of us, wives included, on board his floating palace. What a way to go.

When my wife and I arrived in Fremantle we were greeted by Judy Conner, Roberta Burnham, and Dot Chesebrough. A comfortable townhouse was waiting for us. The Burnhams, Conners, and Whiddens were in the same section. For the first two weeks, designer Bruce Nelson and his sparkling wife Ann shared our dwelling. We were a few short miles from the compound. Fremantle was a friendly and exciting small waterfront town, mainly accommodating the fishing industry and the shipping of sheep. About ten miles away was the modern and beautiful city of Perth.

The first two evenings at our new home, Malin and Dennis discussed the syndicate's financial status, with Dennis stretched out on the floor. I felt the shortfall was greater than it appeared. Malin arranged for Sandy Purdon to bring the books to Fremantle. Meanwhile, we divided a list of names to approach for donations. Each night around 11 p.m. we would make our calls. The following morning, I would collate the results. They were encouraging.

Sandy Purdon and I spent several days reviewing the records, and finally agreed that the program was short several million dollars more than at first realized. This now gave us a target sum which we slowly whittled down. As *Stars & Stripes* continued to win, it became easier to secure the needed funds.

I had no formal title, nor did I need one. At times Malin and Dennis would ask me to perform some special service. Most of the time, I would freely circulate, listen to complaints or suggestions, and then proceed as I would see fit. It was important not to usurp the responsibilities of others. It was not up to me to issue orders. This was a position I was good at. Malin and Dennis were receptive and responsive, and we worked well as an unofficial team.

Venerable Jack Sutphen was the chief "mushroom." The "mushrooms" were an elite group. These were the guys who sailed with Jack on the trial horse. Whenever the opportunity would present itself, they would line up on deck and circle their arms over their heads – the mushroom sign of solidarity and defiance. They even had a large flag which they proudly flew from the headstay. A "mushroom" was defined as being one who was kept in the dark and fed manure. That, obviously, was one of the milder definitions.

When Dennis was about to win the Louis Vuitton trials which would establish *Stars & Stripes* as the official challenger, Commodore Arthur Santry of the NYYC approached me. He was a serious gentleman with a grim approach, and was understandably unhappy about the performance of the eliminated *America II*. He was concerned that Dennis might be drinking too much and cause embarrassment. I assured him that would never be a problem. Although Dennis was under a tremendous strain, he never would conduct himself in a manner that might affect his on-the-water performance. That, I knew from firsthand experience. At first opportunity, which was when Dennis drove me on a sightseeing ride, I discussed Santry's comments with him. He listened but said nothing. He didn't have to. And there never was a problem. On that same drive, a newsboy recognizing Dennis, gave DC a wave and smile. Dennis pulled over, and asked him if he would like to sail on *Stars & Stripes*. WOW! The next day the little Aussie got his ride.

As the pressure mounted, Dennis was upset with the way the press was covering our campaign. One day at our compound, he was talking with the most likable correspondent of all, Walter Cronkite. Suddenly, Dennis walked away without so much as a wave. Walter was taken aback as was I. Dennis' mind was somewhere else.

Dave Knickerbocker, an old friend and sports writer for *Newsday*, invited me to lunch. He explained the problem. The press was unable to talk to Dennis, and were much in the dark concerning our program. Consequently, they would write whatever they could learn secondhand. The result was the publication of often

The entire Freedom squad (including alternates and syndicate principals) outside Seaview Terrace, their "home" in 1980. Many of Newport's famed turn-of-the-century mansions were rented by syndicates during the 12-meter years, creating situations that fostered a family atmosphere.

With Dennis Conner enjoying the ride (below), I'm driving Freedom upwind on a blustery day on Narragansett Bay.

I presented our syndicate flag to Australia II's winning skipper, John Bertrand, in 1983. The official presentation of the Cup that year was a traumatic occasion. America had lost the old mug for the first time in 132 years of competition, and all concerned on the U.S. side were in shock. Our crew was not invited to the presentation.

Another syndicate flag presentation, this one to the Vice-President of the United States. Dennis Conner (left), Fritz Jewett (right) and I did the honors when Vice-President George Bush paid us a visit during the 1983 campaign. Bush became known for his love of fishing from fast power boats, but he was fascinated by America's Cup competition.

In 1983, (from left) our attorney Harman Hawkins, designer Olin Stephens, and the late Arthur Knapp (who skippered Weatherly*) join me for an informal portrait.*

The crew of Enterprise *(1977). Top row, from left: Don Kohlman; Steve Taft; skipper Lowell North; replacement skipper and upwind helmsman Malin Burnham; Roger LeBlanc. Second row, from left: Richard du Moulin; John Marshall; Rod Davis; Em Black; Jim Caldwell; Andy MacGowan. Front row, from left: designer David Pedrick; Fritz Jewett; Ed du Moulin; Olin Stephens.*

A salty shot of me at work (top left) during the 1980 Freedom *campaign.*
A beaten but always gracious Jim Hardy (above), skipper of Australia,
shares a joke with Freedom *skipper Dennis Conner (back to camera).*
Hardy was invited aboard by Conner and given Freedom's *wheel after the*
last race. I'm behind Hardy enjoying the moment.
My late wife Eleanor du Moulin (below) steers Freedom *as skipper Conner*
and syndicate friend Robert Conner (no relation) relax.

President Reagan welcomes Stars & Stripes' sailors at the White House. Our syndicate chairman, Malin Burnham, is at far left. This was the highlight of tumultuous receptions given our team when we returned to the U.S. There was a ticker tape parade up Fifth Avenue in New York, perhaps the first for sailors since the Stephens brothers won the Transatlantic Race in 1931.

Below, the tough boat and ace crew that pulled off the big win on a typical 30-knot afternoon off Fremantle, Western Australia.

Jack Sutphen (at left). The habitual trial horse helmsman was so dedicated to the Cup effort he moved to San Diego from the East Coast.

The hard wing catamaran (top right) used to defend against Michael Fay's rogue challenge in 1988 was the object of much scorn, and started a lawsuit that lasted two years. But it was a brilliant piece of design work, and a technological marvel.

Dennis (right) waves to supporters after making the defender finals in 1992. It was my good luck to sail as 17th man that day.

The late Rod Stephens (left) one of the great seamen of all time, joins me, skipper Dennis Conner, and designer Johan Valentijn for a portrait behind the boom of one of our 12-meters in 1983.

Liberty *(above) sailing upwind off Newport on a moderate day. The boat was no match for* Australia II's *inverted keel with wings. It was a great credit to skipper Dennis Conner and his crew that they were able to force a seventh race.*

Liberty's *afterguard with their manager (left). From left, tactician Tom Whidden; Dennis Conner; me; navigator Halsey Herreshoff; and main trimmer John Marshall.*

In 1987, Dennis and Eleanor share a happy moment
on the airplane bringing the America's Cup back from
Down Under. The Cup is draped in a fur coat given to
Dennis by major syndicate supporter, Bob Aron.
The hat is a gift of then-Australian Prime Minister,
Robert Hawke.

negative and erroneous stories. Dave suggested having Dennis meet with the press, informally, on board *Carmac VI*, before Dennis left for the racecourse. I conveyed this to Malin Burnham who immediately arranged the first of such meetings. Coffee and doughnuts were served. Malin opened the first meeting and then left Dennis with the press. Under such conditions Dennis and the press really got along. No further problems.

We had the best of times on the bridge deck of tender *Betsy* in company with the Jewetts, Jack Sutphen, the capable crew, Dick McCurdy on the computer below, listening to the meteorologist conversing with our weather boats, along with comments from Mort Bloom, our representative on the Race Committee and our rules advisor. The ten minute gun sounded the end of our contact with *Stars & Stripes*. But being on board *Betsy* provided many fond memories.

One of the many kindnesses shown was an invitation from our old adversary from "keelgate," Warren Jones, Alan Bond's project director. He extended an invitation to the *Stars & Stripes* team to view the Superbowl from a large screen set up in their compound. We loved it.

As is so often the case, defeating the Kookaburras was anti-climactic compared to the intensive racing in the challenger trials. The harbor reception we received after each of the Cup races, from both the Australians and Americans lining the rocks, was tremendous. It was doubly so on the day of final victory. Dennis, fearlessly and skillfully sailed *Stars & Stripes* into the wall-to-wall packed harbor under spinnaker without a collision, or even a near miss.

After docking, Dennis came aboard *Betsy*, put his arms around Fritz Jewett and myself. We had an emotional moment which was caught on film. It had been a long road from Newport to Fremantle, from 1983 to 1987.

A Western Australian newspaper wrote: "...very probably the most popular Yank to visit these shores. Conner came to Fremantle as a villain, Big Bad Dennis, and left with the America's Cup in hand as a hero."

Outside our compound after the victory, the crowd was so thick that flag officers of the New York Yacht Club could not get through the police lines to extend their congratulations. When the NYYC had been eliminated, Bill Packer and Art "Capt. Tuna" Wullschleger, *America II*'s general manager and operations director respectively, offered us sails and equipment. We did use one of their spinnakers against *Kookaboura III*. Wullschleger invited me to their compound. It was strange to view various discarded winged keels spread around. I was only too well aware of the effort that each syndicate exerted to win the Cup, and the terrible feeling of being eliminated. The "thrill of victory and the agony of defeat" are experiences that truly do remain with you forever.

The Fremantle restaurants and saloons were hospitable, with fine food and drinks. The American dollar went a long way. A rack of lamb was under $5.00, Australian. Tipping was not permitted. On an early occasion, I left a tip. A few moments later, the waitress ran out into the street to return it to me.

At a party held in the old jailhouse, (300 years before, don't forget, Australia had been settled with prisoners from England), we met a strikingly beautiful woman. My wife told her she looked "smashing." Kerry McManus was editor of *Vogue Magazine of Western Australia*. Before we were to return to the States, the Burnhams, Buzz Schofield, our friend and supporter, Eleanor and I decided to have a farewell party for our Australian friends. We asked Kerry where to have it. Her answer was that it had to be at her home in nearby Peppermint Grove. She insisted and, together with our ladies, arranged for an outstanding evening with music under the stars. Malin and Dennis were delayed as the 12s were late in returning. When we arrived at the McManus' magnificent home, Kerry and her husband Jim told us to greet our guests – their home was ours for the night. Among our guests were Walter Cronkite, Edsel Ford, and former Cup winner Robert Bavier, and many of our stalwart supporters. We had arranged for the installation of permanent lights in the garden as a gift to Kerry and Jim.

It's easy to see why we loved it there. At a press meeting, Dennis was asked about the venue for the next defense. He said he would like it to be Fremantle. The excitement of closing our compound, and attending receptions in honor of our victory, reached a zenith when Prime Minister Robert Hawke spoke after the Cup was handed to Malin and Dennis. His remarkable comments say it all:

"This is one occasion when the Australia Prime Minister speaks for every single Australian when we say to you and your syndicate and your crew, unqualified congratulations on a magnificent achievement."

Continental Airlines flew our team and support group, free of charge, to New York, with victory stops in Hawaii, San Diego, Washington, D.C. What a trip it was! We arrived in Hawaii late, and there was a fine turnout at the airport. By the way, the Cup sat on a first-class seat, wrapped in a long fur coat, sporting a Cup tie, with Hawke's hat – a gift for President Reagan – on the top. Naturally, the safety belt was fastened. The fur coat was a gift from Robert Aron, a major backer. His 75-foot sloop was in our compound. On board had been this same fur coat which Dennis once admired. Bob had promised he would give it to Dennis if he won the America's Cup.

In San Diego, we were given an enthusiastic welcome, a parade, and congratulatory speeches. Malin Burnham and Dennis, native sons, received highest honors. Those of our team who lived in San Diego were smart enough to pick up warm clothes for the trip East. We arrived at our Washington, D.C., hotel at about three in the morning. In spite of the late hour, outside the hotel a full band was playing rousing music. The next morning, before our White House visit, some of our ladies bought warm clothes. It was freezing and our blood was thin from the 100-degree days in Western Australia.

The reception at the White House was impressive. President Reagan and Vice-President Bush gave the team a warm welcome. There were some humorous exchanges between Dennis and the president, particularly when Dennis presented Prime Minister Hawke's hat to President Reagan. Next day, on to New York where Donald Trump had arranged for a Fifth Avenue parade. Was it ever cold… Dennis, wearing his new fur coat, was the only one of us who managed to stay warm. Macy's handed us all woolen hats and gloves. The parade was a great spectacle and another lasting memory. All of us were Trump's luncheon guests at his Grand Hyatt Hotel. Over the weeks ahead we were treated to more ceremonies.

Dennis became a highly marketable hero. No one deserved the rewards more than he. But this had not been a one man show. Each member of the team contributed to the final victory. Malin Burnham was outstanding: cool, relaxed, generous. And as syndicate head, much remained for him to resolve upon his return to San Diego.

This wonderful experience was, all too soon, to be followed by probably the most vitriolic, unhappy episode in America's Cup history: the unexpected and unwelcome challenge from New Zealand.

Author's note: The name of this chapter is intentionally the same as the title of Dennis Conner's book on the 1987 campaign.

CHAPTER 5

THE CAT

ne of my most interesting and challenging roles, during the course of my involvement with the America's Cup, related to the America's Cup of 1988. When Malin Burnham, chairman of the San Diego Yacht Club's Cup defense (Sail America Foundation), first learned of the surprise challenge from the Mercury Bay Boating Club, a little-known boating organization in New Zealand, he called to ask me what I thought of it. My initial reaction was that Michael Fay must be joking. He wasn't, and I could not have been more mistaken.

After *Stars & Stripe*'s victory in 1987 in Fremantle, Western Australia, most Cup followers assumed the next defense would be in the venerable 12-meters "and that all challenges received by a given date would be treated as having been received simultaneously," as Roger Vaughan wrote in *America's Cup XXVII – The Official Record*, a magnificent book.

This was to be San Diego's first defense, and in fact the first defense not conducted by the New York Yacht Club. Historically, just prior to a Cup defense, the New York Yacht Club would announce that if they retained the Cup the next defense would be in 12-meters. At the very moment of victory, they would also engineer the first challenge to ensure that the "challenger of record" would be acceptable to them.

The San Diego Yacht Club was unaware of this clever procedure. Thus, the door was left open for Mr. Fay to become the first challenger, and to set his own terms. The SDYC would be bound to meet that single challenge, thus effectively blocking out any other challengers.

In June, 1987 (only a few months after the SDYC had won the Cup), a meeting

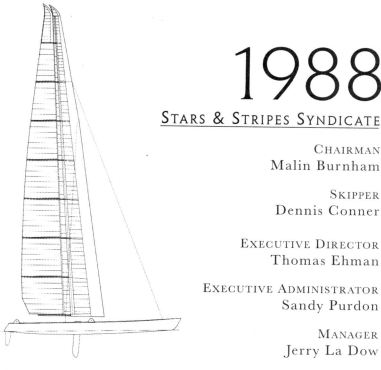

1988

STARS & STRIPES SYNDICATE

CHAIRMAN
Malin Burnham

SKIPPER
Dennis Conner

EXECUTIVE DIRECTOR
Thomas Ehman

EXECUTIVE ADMINISTRATOR
Sandy Purdon

MANAGER
Jerry La Dow

DESIGN TEAM COORDINATOR
John Marshall

DESIGN TEAM
Britton Chance
Dave Hubbard
Duncan MacLane
Bruce Nelson
Bernard Nivelt

BUILDER
R.D. Boatworks (hull)
Scaled Composites (SCI)
(Winged sail)

of the International 12-Metre Association had been held in Porto Cervo, attended by the New Zealanders (including, I believe, Michael Fay), at which the next defense was discussed. While discussing 12-meters, Mr. Fay and associates were in fact carefully studying the Deed of Gift, with the intention of issuing a challenge as set forth in that Deed. Mr. Fay asked Bruce Farr, an outstanding yacht designer, to consider the concept of a very special yacht.

A short time later, the surprise challenge was made, and Farr's design team was ordered to proceed.

While San Diego had been cleaning up its debts from the great 1987 victory of *Stars & Stripes*, the Kiwis were secretly preparing this unexpected challenge. They had a serious jump start, and a monster boat with which to challenge well under way. Fay's *KZ-1*, "the big boat," measured 132 feet overall, 90 feet on the waterline, with a 26-foot beam.

San Diego was in a state of shock after the Kiwi challenge was received. Various discussions were held between San Diego and New Zealand which failed to bring agreement. One counter-proposal of the SDYC was to race with 70-foot waterline length boats, and permit other nations to challenge. This proposal was turned down by the Kiwis who wanted to go one-on-one in 90-foot waterline length mega-yachts. A 90-foot LWL was the maximum, under the Deed, for a *one-*

masted vessel.

Since there was no previous mutual agreement between the challenger and defender, the event would necessarily be governed by the strict wording of the Deed. Now, it was San Diego's turn to carefully read the Deed of Gift. This they did, deciding to fight fire with fire. The issues facing the San Diego Yacht Club were: (1) how to meet this unfriendly and untimely challenge in the most economical and expeditious way possible (within the legal limits of the Deed of Gift), and (2) to successfully defend the Cup.

Of great importance to the SDYC was the challenger letter they had received from New Zealand which expressly stated that there were *no restrictions on design*. This meant that the design restrictions would be dictated only by the Deed of Gift. The door was open for some imaginative solutions.

I often wondered how such a challenge would have been received by another yacht club. Interesting to me was a meeting with the New York Yacht Club's commodore Frank Snyder, granted to me shortly after the New Zealand challenge had been made. After describing the SDYC's developing "catamaran" action (in a manner I thought was convincing), the commodore strongly disagreed with the concept, on the basis of it being unsportsmanlike, in violation of the Deed of Gift, etc. He said the NYYC would never consider such an action. He was later supported by other important members of that club.

A catamaran might be the answer (this was first suggested to me by John Marshall) just as long as it qualified under the Deed of Gift. The $64 question – or much more in this case – had to be answered, and soon. In this atmosphere, Malin Burnham asked if I would head up a "small, fast moving task force" of my own choosing to advise him if, under the Deed, San Diego could respond with such a craft. I agreed, and quickly decided on a three-person committee (including myself). First and foremost, I asked Harman Hawkins, a friend and lawyer, with unmatched experience in Cup and yachting matters, to become the legal arm. In spite of a heavy workload, he accepted on a pro bono basis. I also invited Joanne Fishman, a sportswriter for the *The New York Times*, familiar with yachting and Cup lore and, importantly, an independent thinker. I did not want any "yes men." I convinced Malin that this was a sound combination.

When our group first met, we had a general discussion about the task before us. At the outset, Joanne made a strong argument that a catamaran would be unsportsmanlike and immoral, and she would not support such an idea. Mistakenly, I was convinced that Harman and I could convince her to study the question objectively. Our job was simply to study the Deed, and render an opinion whether *a twin-hull was legal under the Deed of Gift*. It would be up to the SDYC to decide if they wanted to defend in a catamaran. Harman made it clear from the start that what was "within the four corners" of the Deed of Gift would dictate the eligibility of a catamaran.

I was certain that independent legal thinking, countering Joanne Fishman's emotional and non-legal negativity, would give us perfect balance, and trying to convince her to be objective would provide us with every possible argument against the catamaran. Naturally, our study was to be confidential.

To assist us, John Marshall suggested we retain French historian Daniel Charles, who was thoroughly familiar with the Cup and with catamarans. We did, and he proved immensely helpful. We studied many books, not the least of which was Lawson's *History of the Cup*, published in 1901. All in all, we spent over three hundred hours before finalizing our report.

We began a series of interviews, the first with John Marshall, who was brilliant and tough as ever. He was convinced, from the start, that a "cat" would, and should, be the answer. I spoke with the well-respected journalist and yacht designer Bruce Kirby. He suggested we consider a 115-foot LWL, twin-masted vessel. This was clearly allowed in the Deed (and still is). In the early days, schooners were prevalent, and slower than sloops/cutters, hence the additional waterline. But Kirby's idea was quickly discarded as being too costly, and requiring too much time to design and build.

One of the most interesting people interviewed was a true sportsman/gentleman with a vast knowledge of the Cup by heritage and personal experience: Halsey Herreshoff. He was visibly disturbed when we presented the idea of a twin-hulled vessel as a possible defender against the 132-foot challenger. He felt, as Joanne did, that this was unsportsmanlike, and he would have nothing to do with it. Nevertheless, because of our friendship and mutual respect, Halsey agreed to research some of the Herreshoff history of twin-hulled vessels, particularly *Amaryllis*, built in 1876. This *cat* was sailed to the Hudson River from Bristol, Rhode Island, for the purpose of a "match" against a horse and buggy. The latter lost.

Much fuss was made over the perception that a catamaran sailing against a monohull would not be a match, as they were so dissimilar. Many examples of unequal matches were presented. Marshall suggested two adversaries, one with a mace and the other with a broadsword. Other seeming inequities mentioned were the contest (match) between the *Monitor* versus *Merrimac*, and of course, David versus Goliath. But a match, per se, need not be limited to similar design, size, etc. On page 47 of *American Yachts* (1884), I quote, "*Jesse*, a catamaran, beat a race-horse in a long distance match."

Several weeks elapsed before Halsey responded with a nine-page-legal-size-handwritten memo of his thoughts (12/22/87). He urged compromise and a mutual consent approach. He did not rule out a catamaran. Unfortunately, it had become too late for a compromise in spite of efforts made to bring one about.

While our study proceeded, James Michael, a well-respected San Francisco lawyer, active in New York Yacht Club America's Cup matters, published several articles in a yachting publication, taking New Zealand's side. Our Harman Hawkins responded in the same publication. Jim Michael firmly declared a catamaran would and should be declared illegal. I was willing to fly to California to discuss our reasoning with him, but he said that wouldn't be necessary – he would not change his mind. As time went by, the NYYC and Mr. Michael actively gave support to New Zealand, in spite of the fact that the club's original intention was to remain neutral.

ontinuing with our interviews, we turned to P. James Roosevelt, historian of the prestigious Seawanhaka Corinthian Yacht Club. He understood the objective of our study, and gave considerable help. He called our attention to a precedent involving the famous, and still-in-competition, Seawanhaka Cup, which had been established in 1885, the oldest match racing trophy originated in the U.S. Its Deed of Gift was written, based to a large degree, on the America's Cup Deed. In 1898, a challenge came from the Royal St. Lawrence Yacht Club, and much to the surprise of the defending club, a Mr. Duggan arrived with the 35-foot catamaran, *Dominion*. After much argument, the SCYC permitted Mr. Duggan to compete. He did and won, taking the Seawanhaka Cup back to Canada. The Deed, as it had been written, did not disqualify a twin-hull from racing monohulls. The SCYC revised their Deed eliminating future entry of multihulls. The America's Cup Deed of Gift was not so revised.

We learned that the first commodore of the NYYC, John Cox Stevens, had a catamaran in 1819 called *Double Trouble*, which was a failure. In 1877 and 1878, Anson Stokes, a member of the NYYC, entered his *Nereid*, an 82-foot catamaran with elaborate accommodations, in the club's annual cruise. After much argument, the club had to admit her since the rules did not specifically disqualify a multihull. She lost that year and was permitted to compete again the following year, losing once again to the monohulls.

John Rousmaniere, well-known author of books about the sea and historian for the NYYC, had a deep-seated concern about sportsmanship, fair play, and a firm belief that the two competitors had to be equally matched. Here again, emotions ruled over legality.

Simplified, "mismatch" was the cornerstone of Michael Fay's (later Sir Michael Fay) eventual lawsuit. "Match," as defined in the Deed of Gift, seemed very broad, in that "any organized yacht club of a foreign country...shall always be entitled to the right of sailing a match for the Cup...against any yacht or vessel constructed in the country holding the Cup." As mentioned earlier, Fay's challenge expressly stated conditions which established that there were to be no design restrictions other than as specified in the Deed.

Cup history shows that fairness and sportsmanship were not always practiced by the defending club. The first two defenses, against English challengers, were publicly denounced as "unfair and unsportsmanlike." In the first defense in 1870, an entire NYYC squadron of yachts met the lone challenger. Recognizing the unfairness, George Schuyler had the Deed changed so that, in the future, only one boat should face the challenger at a time. In 1871, England again challenged. This time the NYYC had four yachts ready to meet the challenger – some for light weather, others for heavy weather. Actually two different vessels were used, *Sappho* and *Livonia*, in separate races against the single challenger. Again, a cry of unsportsmanlike conduct resulted in George Schuyler revising the Deed once more, creating a one boat versus one boat match race. In each of these cases, the NYYC insisted that the challenger had to accept the conditions set forth in the Deed. Here, 118 years later, the San Diego Yacht Club felt the public's outcry. This time, since there was no prior mutual agreement between the challenging and defending clubs, the contest had to be governed by the strict wording within the limits of the Deed.

Prior to the conclusion of our committee's study, and to my considerable disappointment, Joanne Fishman openly threw her lot in with the NYYC and the New Zealanders. Harman Hawkins and I presented our report to Malin Burnham. It was in brief form. Our conclusion was that the SDYC, if they so wished, could defend in a catamaran within the Deed of Gift. We explained that the vote of our committee was two to one, giving recognition to the dissenting viewpoint of Mrs. Fishman.

Ultimately, this was the first Cup defense that was fought both on the water and in court. The first court decision gave the Cup to New Zealand. On appeal, it was reversed. Then the court ruled that New Zealand and San Diego should go ahead and race; that a final decision would be made later. This upset much of the international yachting community. Could the court upset the race results after the race took place? The answer was yes. Eventually, the case ended in the New York Court of Appeals (that state's highest court). The Court of Appeals declined to rule on sportsmanship, but stated that the race was perfectly legal under the Deed of Gift.

To our great relief, *Stars & Stripes*, San Diego's defending catamaran with Dennis Conner as skipper, became the successful Cup defender. In passing, one could consider that the defender might have been a trimaran or a 115-foot LWL twin-masted vessel, as Bruce Kirby had suggested, and still come within the requirements of the Deed of Gift.

To backtrack a little, John Marshall, who so successfully led the 1987 design team, once again had assumed that role. This time, as the interest centered around a catamaran, John secured the services of top catamaran experts like Duncan MacLane and Carl Hubbard, who were very familiar with the Little America's Cup C-Cats. Bruce Nelson and Britton Chance, part of John's 1987 design team, were also on board. Cam Lewis and Randy Smyth, top catamaran racers, were recruited. Additionally, Gino Morelli and Bernard Nivelt, specialists in the design and construction of cats, rounded out this awesome and unique team that brought mono- and multi-hull experts together on the same project.

They were working against time. The team went to work in the Mojave Desert, of all places, where Scaled Composites was located. This company had constructed the fantastic ultra-light airplane, *Voyager*, which had successfully circled the globe non-stop.

It was decided to build two catamarans, one with a wing sail, and the other a soft sail. Dennis was preparing himself by sailing a souped-up 40-foot cat, while the designers and builders were hard at work. Once Dennis capsized, and his picture appeared in the local papers and various magazines standing on an upturned pontoon. Criticism poured in. "Isn't he smart enough to let a Cam Lewis or a Randy Smyth be the skipper?" was the cry. After all, what does Dennis know about a catamaran? I called Dennis, who calmly told me that he and his crew had been and still were testing various breaking points, and had increased the height of the mast to see how far they could go. This had been exactly Dennis' strategy when he sailed *Freedom* in well over 30 knots shortly before the 1980 defense.

Dennis sailed each of the newly built catamarans, one against the other. I had the pleasure and thrill of sailing with Dennis on both. In a wind of 12 knots, we would exceed 20 knots of speed. The hard sail (108 feet tall and as large as a Boeing 707 wing) was privately favored. However, when Dennis sailed the cat with the hard sail, he would intentionally slow her down.

The actual America's Cup sail-off against the monstrous New Zealand challenger presented a foregone conclusion. The biggest concern was the possibility of heavy winds and seas, in which case the ultra-light defender would be in serious danger of falling apart. There was no way to reef *US 1*. Plans were drawn whereby a top section of the mast could be removed as a means of reducing sail area.

However, such plans were shelved.

Another example of the ingenuity of the team related to a method of storing the winged-sail catamaran on the shore at night. The danger of a strong wind striking the wing in an upright position was too risky to allow it to remain upright when hauled. A clever cradle called the "Tiltmobile" was built, on which the cat would be placed, secured, and then rotated until the wing was parallel to the ground. It was very convenient for those who had to repair, revise, and clean *US 1*. And it was safe.

Other than the striking and unusual sight of two ultra-modern vessels racing (more like an exhibition) over the course of 15 miles to windward, 15 miles to leeward, as dictated by the Deed of Gift, there was little excitement on the water. Broadcasters Gary Jobson and Jim Kelly, joined by the experienced and knowledgeable Tom Blackaller, did their best to make their commentaries exciting. For me, on the water, the scenes were occasionally interesting, but the racing was, frankly, boring. The real battle for this America's Cup would be in the courtrooms.

The ultimate court success in this most contentious challenge came as a result of the hard work of the officers of the SDYC, Sail America's trustees, the law firm of Latham & Watkins, along with the outstanding counsel of Harman Hawkins. I did my part. While doing so, I had the gratifying experience of learning much more about the America's Cup and the vagaries of human nature.

Unlike on other contentious occasions, the Deed of Gift was not changed as a result of this challenge. For a time following the campaign, it seemed that the San Diego Yacht Club and the New York Yacht Club would update the Deed. This never came to pass.

The successful 1988 defense was nothing to be proud of, as it was a contest of unevenly matched yachts. As far as sportsmanship went, it was not a shining moment. However, it was a seminal point in the history of the America's Cup. The San Diego Protocol of 1992 did result from this challenge and defense, and constructively established procedures to keep the America's Cup out of the courts in the future. It succeeded in doing so in 1992, 1995, and 2000. Another exciting action led to the replacement of the great but dated 12-meter boats, by the creation of a new International America's Cup Class (IACC), which brought even greater international participation for the world's oldest sporting trophy.

This aberration, this seagoing match between David and Goliath, did not, as many doomsayers thought, serve to lessen the world's interest in the America's Cup. Quite the contrary.

CHAPTER **6**

ESCALATION

uch good came out of the 1988 controversial catamaran defense of the Cup. The San Diego Protocol established a Trustee's Committee in September, 1988, that included the commodores of the three yacht clubs which had won the Cup: New York, Royal Perth, and San Diego. This committee would settle all differences in the future, and thus avoid court action.

On-the-water umpires were introduced. They would eliminate the long hours of settling protests on shore. In Fremantle (1987), the frequent and lengthy evening protest meetings had been onerous to everyone. Lawyers had been retained by some of the contestants who were constantly at each other's throats. Certain issues, like a 1992 Italian protest against New Zealand relating to her bowsprit, was handled ashore by a jury since it was not an incident relating to tactics on the water. Other than a few controversial calls, the system was to prove effective.

After the catamaran-versus-big boat "mismatch" in 1988, the predicted loss of interest in the America's Cup did not materialize. Far from it. In the 1992 contest, of the original 21 challenging groups from 14 nations, eight survived to challenge. Of an original 11, only two American syndicates actually competed for the right to defend.

This historical record number of challenges can be attributed to the San Diego Protocol which eliminated the "pocket challenges" used by the New York Yacht Club for so many years. The Protocol stated that all challenges received within six months of the last race would be accepted equally. From amongst themselves, all properly accredited challengers would then have the opportunity to select the Challenger of Record. They also would establish by "mutual con-

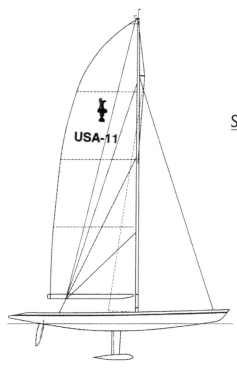

USA-11

1992

STARS & STRIPES SYNDICATE

CHAIRMAN / SKIPPER
Dennis Conner

EXECUTIVE DIRECTOR
Jerry La Dow

OPERATIONS MANAGER
Bill Trenkle

DESIGN TEAM
David Pedrick
Bruce Nelson
Dr. Alberto Calderon

BUILDER
Eric Goetz

sent" the number of races, type of boat, courses, etc.

A new racecourse of 22.6 nautical miles, consisting of eight legs, including a "Z" (two reaching legs) configuration and a downwind finish, was adopted and the old America's Cup course retired. This new course was designed to give spectators and television viewers more action. The hairpin turn at the bottom of the Z was a complicated maneuver. Other than this possibility for some excitement at the mark, the leg proved to be a boring parade, and the additional sails required cost a great deal. For the 1995 defense, the two reaching legs – the Z – were eliminated.

Of greatest impact was the adoption of a new class designed to replace the 12-meter yachts that had been used from 1958 to 1987. Early in September of 1988, a meeting was held at the San Diego Yacht Club attended by over 20 designers and others closely involved in the Cup. The chairman was William Ficker, America's Cup Hall of Famer and skipper of the 1967 Cup defender *Intrepid*. The press was excluded, perhaps to ensure an open and frank discussion among those present.

It certainly was a no-holds-barred meeting. Everyone had a chance to speak. The multi-hull supporters urged that consideration be given to adopting a multi-hull class. Some urged an updated 12-meter with a taller rig. The representatives from the smaller countries opted for the updated 12-meter. Ultra-light displacement boats (ULDB) were suggested. However, the heavy pressure came from Alan Bond and Michael Fay who pushed for a 90-foot LWL ($4 million plus) vessel. It was obvious the time for a change had arrived. A compromise was reached with a 75-foot LOA boat. A meeting was set for October in England for the designers to establish guidelines for this new class.

Ultimately, the International America's Cup Class (IACC) was adopted. The average boat would be 75-foot LOA, 57-foot LWL, beam of 18 feet, draft of 13 feet. The sail area would be increased to 7,500 square feet versus the 4,500 square feet of the 12s, yet the displacement would be only 37,000 pounds, versus 56,000 pounds for the smaller 12s.

In addition to a crew of 16 sailors, five more than the 12s required, rules permitted an observer on board during the races. This became known as the "17th man," or to be more "politically correct," a "17th person." Before the defense was over, 28 IACC's would have been built at an estimated cost of $2,000,000 each.

Thus, the 12-meters, after 34 years of exciting competition culminating in the fantastic contest off Fremantle, Western Australia, were retired into America's Cup history. The IACC's held their first World Championships in San Diego waters May 4-11, 1991. Nine of the new class entered. It was an exciting regatta. Before it ended, there would be plenty of damage (exceeding a million dollars) while crews were familiarizing themselves with this ultra-modern design. It was this "demolition derby" that prompted William Koch to criticize this design as dangerous and ridiculous.

Dennis Conner's *Stars & Stripes* was followed closely. In spite of a sparse sail inventory, *Stars & Stripes* was one of the top four qualifiers. However, Dennis withdrew from the finals, making room for the Japanese. This was a practical move based on lack of equipment and the more pressing need for him to devote his time to fundraising.

The two American syndicates which would compete for the right to defend for the San Diego Yacht Club were led by Dennis Conner (Mr. America's Cup) and by William Koch, a near-billionaire who had started sailing in a big way only eight years before. The only way Koch knew how to do things was his way, and full speed ahead. He was a great believer that if properly applied, science would be key to his reaching his goal. Bill Koch ignored all those who scoffed at his dream (as most everyone did). He planned to compete in the spirit of pure Corinthian sportsmanship and avoid any commercialism. In a February, 1991, interview appearing in *SAILING* magazine, he talked of a Cup "with amateurs" and of having "a completely clean boat with no sponsors' logos" and "the chance to do it with style and integrity." His intentions were good but quite naïve. Further, he darkly alluded to "viciousness and cutthroat attitudes on the race course." To succeed, Bill would have to learn the "facts of life." In responding to the article, I pointed out that "cutthroat competition is not necessarily wrong or a sign of poor sportsmanship, but more a reflection of the competitive spirit of many of our sailing luminaries..." He became a fast learner as he soon had to face the realities of experienced campaigners such as Dennis Conner and Paul Cayard. Ted Turner and the late Tom Blackaller also surely qualified as formidable cutthroat America's Cup veterans.

Eventually, Koch sought corporate backing and did allow logos on his boats. He also developed a record payroll. So much for the "pure Corinthian" amateurs. He hired a number of sailing "rock stars" (excellent sailors with high profiles) like Buddy Melges, Gary Jobson, John Kostecki, and the late Larry Klein. But Bill was definitely "The Boss." It was his money, it was his show. He would take an active part in the onboard leadership and he did some steering, mostly downwind. The highly respected and humorous Buddy Melges was to be his main helmsman, and Dave Dellenbaugh would be his starting helmsman. Would this work? It didn't in 1977 when Lowell North, Malin Burnham, and John Marshall shared the helm of *Enterprise*. Dave Dellenbaugh was to outshine Paul Cayard on the starting line in the actual defense and deserves a large share of credit for Koch's on-the-water success.

Everyone was critical of Bill's crew organization. He stubbornly chose not to designate a skipper until late in the game. Gary Jobson resigned, Larry Klein resigned, as did John Kostecki. It was Buddy Melges who held the remaining crew together, and should receive much of the credit for the ultimate victory. On February 27, 2001, at the New York Yacht Club, it was announced that Buddy Melges would be one of the next three inductees into the America's Cup Hall of Fame. His induction would take place at Cowes, England, during the 150th Jubilee of the America's Cup, to be held in August, 2001.

During the shuffling of the cockpit stars, Britton Chance even suggested a scenario with Dennis Conner at the helm of Koch's *America* [3]. Bill was determined and thick-skinned. He took a lot of punishment, but remained steadfast in his beliefs.

Never before had anyone spent the money Bill did on a defense. Four IACC boats were built for his campaign. His budget was estimated to be $65 million of which probably $50 million came from his coffers. Amazingly, this was exceeded by the Italian challenge led by the late Raul Gardini (Montedison) that spent about $100 million and built five IACC boats. Such massive campaigns, not surprisingly, led to limitations being set for future Cup campaigns. Dennis Conner spent about $10 million for his one-boat effort. To jump ahead a bit, for the year 2000 Cup defense, Dennis had a similar budget and one boat. And yet, Dennis' *Stars & Stripes* came very close to making the finals in Auckland.

Dennis had considered building a second boat for the 1992 races. He is an outstanding fund raiser, and public awareness of the Cup was high, but corporate interest was at a low point, partly resulting from the long drawn out legal battle lasting almost 18 months after the catamaran's successful defense in 1988. The decision was not handed down by the highest court in New York State until April 26, 1990. This delay made it extremely difficult to secure sufficient major corporate backing. It gave the foreign challengers a substantial head start on design and fund raising.

Under the leadership of the always imaginative and energetic John Marshall, a fund of $1,000,000 was raised to start working on the defender design, which was to be shared by both American syndicates. This was a first, and brought into existence the Partnership for America's Cup Technology (PACT).

Dennis' pursuit of corporate support took a real toll on his energy and time. He commuted to the East Coast and spent long hours selling his program. No one knew better than Dennis that a one-boat effort to win the America's Cup was highly unlikely to succeed. (This would be proved once again by the survival of *AmericaOne* and *Prada*, both two-boat syndicates that squared off in the Louis Vuitton finals in New Zealand, January, 2000.)

uring a visit to San Diego before the 1992 series, Dennis and I discussed his alternatives. To build a second boat would force him to borrow money. Going into debt was something he would never do. My comment to him was that a one-boat losing effort would be more likely to enhance his reputation than to harm it. There was no doubt in my mind that Team Dennis Conner would put up a terrific fight with the one new boat. It would be the oldest boat in competition, having been launched in the spring of 1991. Being the underdog is not new to Dennis, and it is a role he finds quite comfortable. I helped where I could, working closely with his staff, raising funds from his loyal supporters of past campaigns.

It was my good fortune to have been the 17th man on *Stars & Stripes* when she beat Koch's *Kanza*, and thus entered the Defender Finals in 1992. Had *Stars & Stripes* defended, Italy probably would have won the Cup, as the winds during the defense were considerably higher than the light winds favorable to *Stars & Stripes*. But with Dennis, you never know.

The point system adopted for the Defender Trials was complicated and gave an advantage to Koch. He could manipulate crews and boats to get the most favorable points. His game plan called for eliminating Dennis from the Final Trials. In such an event, Koch would have his own two boats to fight it out for the right to be the defender, a no-lose situation. Dennis' qualifying for the final trials turned out to be fortuitous for the American defense effort. It certainly better prepared Koch for his successful defense against *Il Moro Di Venezia* skippered by Paul

Cayard. You can be sure that it sharpened Dave Dellenbaugh's starting capabilities, having to compete first against "The Master."

Dennis managed to maintain a friendly relationship with Bill Koch. They would spend some evenings together socially. Bill had rented a beautiful house on the water near the San Diego Yacht Club, not far from the house that the Conners rented. Koch is a collector of important art. He had shipped to San Diego, from his home in the East, a number of valuable and very large Botero sculptures. Most talked about was the voluptuous "fat lady with a cigar" lying nude on her stomach on his front lawn and known generally as Roseanne. Bill had a 24-hour guard protecting his home and the lawn sculptures. Each morning, Dennis and a group of us would pass Koch's house around 6:00 a.m. Dennis would call out "Good morning, Bill." Bill would usually respond in a sleepy voice. One day a brassiere was hung on Roseanne's ample bosom. On another occasion, a *Stars & Stripes* banner hung from her neck.

Dennis, not to be outdone by the Boteros, displayed on his waterfront lawn two scroungy ersatz lions guarded by a shapely, bikini-clad girl mannikin wearing a large sheriff's hat and badge on a bosom not quite as ample as Roseanne's.

At one point, Bill and Dennis discussed a possible alliance, for which Dennis would receive substantial payment. It would have required Dennis to join Koch's effort without his crew, and that Dennis would not do. They would have made an interesting combination: Bill, with his money and an oft-repeated motto – "Talent, Teamwork and Technology" – and Dennis' "No Excuse to Lose" attitude and his proven capabilities in handling a crew and getting the most out of a boat. But it was not to be – then or later.

William Koch was determined to do what he wanted. And what he wanted comprised some true America's Cup innovations: he was the first Cup skipper to have an African American on board a defender. Dawn Riley was the first woman actually to work as crew on a defender, not in an afterguard. In the golden age of the America's Cup, some wives of skippers/owners had in fact served as timekeepers or observers. The biggest surprise was to come in his next campaign. In 1995, Koch created the "All Girl Crew," which later, of course, became the "Almost All Girl Crew."

As one might expect of a man with unlimited resources, the 1992 Koch compound was outstanding. His crew and support staff exceeded 200 people. The facilities included a first-rate area for physical conditioning and therapy. The compound was under heavily guarded security, even for crew members, and boasted the finest equipment.

Comparison with Team Dennis Conner was startling. The latter's compound was extremely modest with makeshift facilities for comfort, a crowded trailer-like office, and a small but dedicated and capable support staff.

For *Stars & Stripes*, the design team of Dave Pedrick, Alberto Calderon, and Bruce Nelson complemented one another. They worked ceaselessly to squeeze more speed from Dennis' one "old" boat. It was Calderon who, in 1987, had led the experiment on St. Francis Yacht Club's *USA 1* skippered by Tom Blackaller. *USA 1* sported three foils on her underbody: forward rudder, after rudder, ballast bulb suspended in between struts, in place of a keel. *USA 1* was before her time, but had worried the opposition nonetheless.

During a crucial second round series, a radical twin keel with no aft rudder was installed on *Stars & Stripes*, steering being accomplished by forward and aft trim tabs. The first day she raced with these appendages, I watched along with others from the bridge of tender *Betsy* while *Stars & Stripes* was going upwind. She seemed to be going sideways faster than forward. That day, *Stars & Stripes* lost by six disheartening minutes.

That night, and in an impressive 14 hours, the hardworking shore team changed her back to the old keel, and replaced her mast. Next day, *Stars & Stripes* went out and won – with thanks to Bill Koch for permitting the change in mid-round.

America[3] won in a very competitive contest. It was not as easy as the four-to-one results would make one believe.

The Koch program included an elaborate "spy" operation, including having a diver photograph the underbody of a competitor, while swimming near a turning mark. It probably wasn't as sophisticated a program as the competition believed. It did add to the mystique and to the lore of the Cup, as well as contributing to a ruling which would, in future events, limit costs and publicly disclose the underbodies before the main event.

"Spritgate," another 1992 campaign hiccup, uncovered a problem of contradictory actions by two juries. For the Louis Vuitton Challenger Series, there was one jury; there was also the America's Cup International Jury. The AC Jury, with no jurisdiction over the Louis Vuitton series, was asked its opinion on the Kiwi practice of attaching the gennaker sheet to the bowsprit. Their opinion was that it was a violation. The Louis Vuitton jury chose to ignore it. In the fateful final round, with the score four-to-one in New Zealand's favor, Paul Cayard protested *NZL 20*. The Louis Vuitton jury decided to cancel the race, thus setting the score back to three-to-one. New Zealand conformed. This distraction combined with a change in skippers resulted in the Italians winning the next three races, and thus *Il Moro Di Venezia* became the challenger.

This distraction upset the leading Kiwis. They were demoralized. The result was a last minute skipper change (Rod Davis to Russell Coutts) for *NZL* with its two trim tabs and no rudder. It could not have been easy for Coutts to become familiar with the steering of *NZL* on such short notice. Some suggested it would have been smarter to have Coutts start and Davis steer. Great opportunity for the second guessers. I was reminded of *Liberty*, with its three-to-one lead in 1983, only to eventually end up losing four-to-three to *Australia II*.

When Rod Davis was replaced, I remembered that time when a younger Rod Davis had broken down upon hearing that his hero Lowell North had been replaced as skipper of *Enterprise*. Now, 15 years later, Rod was to go through this traumatic experience himself. I felt badly for him, particularly since he had performed so well. But it never did slow him down. He continues to serve in important America's Cup roles, including that of coach for the *Prada* challenge of 2000.

America ³ successfully defended the America's Cup. Bill Koch succeeded in doing it his way. What America's Cup campaign isn't full of surprises?

CHAPTER 7

REVERSAL

fter the successful defense in 1992, the San Diego Yacht Club dele-
gated the responsibility of being the event organizer to a newly
formed America's Cup '95 Committee.

Initially, there were ten challenges from seven countries. This
would decrease to seven from five countries. On the defense side, the
participation of Bill Koch, the 1992 successful defender, was unde-
cided. His elaborate compound remained in excellent condition. But Bill had personal legal problems and had voiced his dislike of past San Diego Yacht Club
treatment, real or imagined. Meanwhile, Dennis Conner, under the banner of
Team Dennis Conner, announced his intention to participate in the defense. The
veteran John Marshall decided he would form his own syndicate, PACT'95, along
with Kevin Mahaney, an Olympic silver medalist from Maine. Finally, in May
1994, William Koch threw his hat into the ring. Koch's America[3] team, familiarly
known as the "Cubens," would return.

To an astonished world, Koch announced that he would build a new boat to
be manned by women only, so to speak. Once again, as in the 1992 program, Bill
Koch was going to do it his way. To the cynical sailing world this break with the
143-year-old male domination of the America's Cup was a ridiculous program
destined to be a dismal failure. In the 1930s, several wives of Cup
challengers/defenders had served in the afterguard as timekeepers or observers,
but never as crew until Dawn Riley sailed with Koch's program in 1992.

A team of topnotch, dedicated, and athletic women was recruited. They were
enthusiastic and, except for Riley, had no Cup experience. The women trained
hard and, to everyone's amazement, performed as well as any of the crews in the

USA-34

1995

STARS & STRIPES SYNDICATE

CHAIRMAN / MANAGER
Dennis Conner

SKIPPER
Paul Cayard

OPERATIONS MANAGER
Bill Trenkle

DESIGNER
David Pedrick

BUILDER
Eric Goetz

YOUNG AMERICA USED
TO DEFEND AMERICA'S CUP

DESIGNER
Bruce Nelson

BUILDER
Eric Goetz

competitive IACC World's Championships in 1994, coming in a surprising second to *OneAustralia*. This was even more remarkable given the relatively short training period they had to prepare themselves. They began practice in May, 1994, and didn't start to sail on the new *Mighty Mary* until right before the Citizen's Cup defender trials Round Robin 4 (early March, 1995). They endured many heavy tacking duels, which are very physically taxing, beating *Stars & Stripes* at times as well as *Young America*. They became the center of attraction. My wife and I knew many of the crew, and Eleanor enthusiastically rooted for them even though we were part of the Conner team.

I could not help but be reminded of this special group while watching the exciting World's Women's Soccer Championships in July, 1999. The women from *Mighty Mary* set the pace.

The Koch syndicate's new boat was named Mighty Mary, after Koch's mother. It was an interesting gesture given that he was involved in a lawsuit against her.

PACT '95 hired Bruce Nelson to design their new IACC. They concentrated heavily on technology, and had behind them the invaluable SAIC. Their new boat *Young America* was painted from a design by the famous artist Roy Lichtenstein: a comely mermaid stretched the length of the hull. It was quite a shock to the establishment, but striking it was. It represented another break with tradition. With logos, even on Mr. Koch's IACCs, what was the world of the America's Cup coming to?

Dennis ordered a new boat designed by David Pedrick. This was *US34* in which he practiced against the 1992 *US11*. The old *Stars & Stripes* was fifth out of seven in the 1994 Worlds, but San Diego's local hero stole the show during the exhibition races held in San Diego Harbor. Under full sail, he entered one of the pier areas, and within a few yards of the bulkhead and a cheering crowd, sailed agilely out.

Dennis was carrying a full load as syndicate manager, chief fund raiser, and skipper. Paul Cayard was to be his helmsman, a man Dennis had competed against in various class boats (Star boats especially) over many years. Each admired the other but they were definitely fierce competitors. In the days when Paul teamed up with the charismatic Tom Blackaller, they always tried to intimidate Dennis. This was now a more mellow Paul Cayard.

For a time Paul's starts were not too inspiring. Dennis was urged to do the starts himself but he would not upstage or second guess Paul. Dennis knew how to conduct himself, and he let Paul run the boat. They made a fine team. Paul was welcomed on board by the entire crew. It was a satisfying experience to watch them all work so well together.

Unfortunately, *Stars & Stripes* appeared to be the slowest of the American boats. The fact that they eliminated the two other contenders is a testimonial to the caliber of the team both ashore and afloat.

In 1995 Dennis invited me once again to help and I did some fund raising, worked behind the scenes, and rode the tender. However, this was a different Dennis. This was not the hands-on Dennis I knew. He arrived at the compound later and departed earlier. As usual, he had capable people around him. Jerry La Dow and Bill Trenkle, in particular, carried heavy loads. The crew meetings were few and far between. Dennis had gone through a quiet divorce and now was married to an attractive young woman. He seemed distracted. In the past, his mind had been firmly fixed on his campaigns, with family and business taking back seats.

In the America's Cup of 1992 many changes were made to level the playing field, reduce costs, and make it more exciting for the spectators. I believe these goals were largely achieved. By eliminating the Z reaching legs there was a sizable reduction in the cost of sails while doing away with the boring game of "follow the leader." And a syndicate would not be permitted to build more than two new boats. Once again, we heard the all too familiar cry of "unfair" when two Australian syndicates, each with two boats, announced they were going to work together. This controversy lasted from August, 1994, to December before it was settled in Australia's favor.

In 1992, spying had gotten out of hand. Bill Koch used a special spy boat which got under the skin of the opposition. After the '92 campaign was over, we learned that it was primarily used for weather observations. Koch had also hired divers to photograph competitors' underwater foils as they rounded a mark of the race-course. Small craft had come dangerously close alongside to observe a competitor. In any event, such activities were substantially curtailed for future defenses.

Under the new rules, after the final trials every syndicate would have to remove security skirts to allow the world to view their boats' underwater appendages. On Feb 4, 1995, keels were unveiled to much fanfare and excitement. First *Young America* undraped, followed by *Stars & Stripes*. In the late afternoon, an immense and enthusiastic crowd gathered at the New Zealand compound to view *NZL*'s design. The two narrow New Zealand boats looked as impressive as their sailing records.

The starting line was reduced in length by half. Pre-start maneuvers were reduced to five minutes from 10, starboard roundings were introduced, the course distance was shortened to 18.55 nautical miles with windward and leeward legs only. In 1992, there had been two juries. In the bowsprit controversy ("Spritgate"), they arrived at different conclusions. Now, there would be only one International Jury. For the first time, both the defender and challenger would announce their boats at the same time, an important concession to the challenger. Prior to this, the challenger had to select his boat at the start of his trials, while the defender could wait until right before the Cup races began. Most of these changes were for the better from a cost point of view as well as the spectator/television viewpoint. And, of course, from the fairness perspective.

The defense budgets ran from $15 million to $20 million, a far cry from Koch's $60 million and Guardini's $100 million in 1992. The San Diego Yacht Club along with Royal Perth and New York deserve much credit for the budget reduction, and the leveling of the playing field. Following the bitterness of the 1988 campaign, both were welcome changes.

In spite of Bill Koch's repeated and vehement denials that there ever would be a man on board *Mighty Mary*, including a video taped statement to Jim Kelly (ESPN) just a few days before, Koch unabashedly changed his mind. He said he felt it came down to a question of either elimination or the addition of one sea-soned male with America's Cup experience (one particularly adept on the starting line). One of *Mighty Mary*'s coaches, the modest and unassuming Dave Dellenbaugh, was the person in mind. Bill met with his team and they supported the move. The heaviest blow fell on J.J. Isler. As a team player, the able J.J. stepped aside and demonstrated real character by sailing the second boat against *Mighty Mary*. Dave became known as the "The Bearded Lady." He took over as starting helmsman and tactician. There was a tremendous outburst of public criticism. Koch had to placate his sponsors. He never wavered.

As with every defense, contentious issues would arise. Near disasters and actual disasters would occur. The 29th Defense had plenty of both.

There was the dropping of *France 2* onto a concrete surface and, three months later, her spectacular capsize when her keel fell off. A few days before her commissioning, on January 5, 1995, a tornado badly damaged *Young America*. On March 12, *Young America* had a second calamity. While being towed out of Mission Bay, she fell off a nine-foot wave and suffered considerable damage. Just before the start of a challenger race in Round Robin 2, the 94,000-ton aircraft carrier *Abraham Lincoln* appeared out of a dense fogbank at the starting line, scaring everyone including those on the carrier's bridge. The race was called off. On March 26, *Stars & Stripes* almost sank when she sustained a fracture in the keel area. Working through the night, a dedicated shore support team replaced her keel (and mast). She was launched the next morning, and won her race that day.

March 5, 1995 was a day to remember. It became known as "Black Sunday." It was an overcast, rainy day with winds of 20 knots and a lumpy sea. John Bertrand questioned whether it was a suitable day for racing. The conditions were within the rule of thumb but on the outer edge. The decision to race was made. Prior to the start, *Stars & Stripes'* Ralf Steitz lost his grip while working up the mast and dangled dangerously, upside down in a bos'n chair 100 feet above the deck, in the rough seas. He was rescued by a shipmate. Halfway up the weather leg of the race, *OneAustralia*, winner of the IACC World Championship, suddenly bent amidships. The headsail began to flutter, and the stern bent up as if to meet the bow. She was sinking. The crew leapt overboard, and in less than three minutes *OneAustralia*'s masthead disappeared. The hull came to rest on the bottom 500 feet below. New Zealand's rubber chase boat lost no time in helping to rescue all hands. For the first time in the 144 year history of the America's Cup, a contender had sunk. That same day, *Mighty Mary* experienced gear failure, and *France III* lost her mast.

Who says sailboat racing is like watching grass grow? Was Bill Koch right in labeling the IACC boats as too dangerous?

One of the most discussed issues arose at the very height of the excitement. The American trials were about over. *Young America* had the best record. *Stars & Stripes*, with the worst record, was to race *Mighty Mary*. Whichever team lost would be *out*. But there was a deal in the offing.

The issue was whether an agreement by mutual consent could be made to extend the American defender trials. It's unclear who dreamed this up, but sponsor fulfillment could have provided a major impetus. A longer set of trials would mean more media coverage, which in turn would mean happier sponsors. And more preparation through competition would not hurt America's chances in the actual Cup races. There was great concern that *NZL* was more than a worthy challenger, having lost but two races all season. And one of those was lost in the protest room for allowing a crewman to stand on the highest spreader, seeking out wind shifts. When *NZL* heeled, the crewman was outside the deck perimeter, a rule violation.

And so the night before *Stars & Stripes* do-or-die race against *Mighty Mary*, the three syndicate heads vying for the right to defend the Cup sat down and tried to hammer out a deal that would extend the final trials, and include all three boats. All three syndicate crews knew what was up, and supported their bosses' efforts. But at 10:30 that evening, John Marshall, Bill Koch, and Dennis Conner adjourned with no agreement in place. Next morning, however, they reconvened, ironed out differences, and struck a deal. Unique at best in the annals of Cup competition, the deal was mostly viewed as outrageous. But it was quickly approved by the San Diego Yacht Club's America's Cup Defense Committee.

Marshall, head of PACT '95, was confident that his syndicate's boat – *Young America* – would be the defender, given its outstanding record. To ensure having the inside track, and after a series of scientific calculations, John Marshall, who usually gets what he wants, negotiated two points for his team going into the extended three-way Final Trials. *Mighty Mary* got one point and *Stars & Stripes*, with the poorest record, no points. Dennis didn't argue. "After analyzing this, it was our conclusion that you can't fight if you're dead," Dennis said with a smile at the press conference the next day.

Stars & Stripes and *Mighty Mary* raced that same day. Dennis' crew knew of the newly crafted arrangement, but Bill Koch decided not to tell his team. He wanted to see how they acted under "kill or be killed" conditions. The mostly women's team, as usual, sailed aggressively to win, probably more so with the stakes so high, and win they did by the astonishing time of five minutes 59 seconds. Their exuberance was dampened when they were told that the race did not count. Their shock and dismay was captured by ESPN's cameras. But they would survive this terrible disappointment. Along with many others, I thought this was a cruel hoax.

Stars & Stripes was still alive. Dennis Conner, often blamed for rocking the boat, was unfairly accused of engineering this unprecedented rule change, thus extending the trials. Dave Dellenbaugh, in an article "Confessions of the Bearded Lady" (Oct '95 *SAIL*), said that "Dennis did not cheat or manipulate his way into the defender finals. The three-way agreement was made within the rules, and agreed to by the three syndicates." Dennis had nothing to lose with the slowest boat among the defenders.

The best was yet to come.

The final Finals were now at hand. Suddenly *Stars & Stripes* came alive, and began to win. In spite of the handicap, she posted the best record: six wins and two losses. The last race of the Citizens Final made the record book. At the last windward mark *Mighty Mary* led by over 40 boat lengths – four minutes, eight seconds – and the final leg was only three miles long. Everyone assumed that had to be the end. Even the television broadcast came to an end. *Stars & Stripes* was *out* at last. But…in the very light, unsettled weather, Conner found his own private breeze, and suddenly *Mighty Mary*'s lead was cut in half. Spooked by the onrushing *Stars & Stripes*, the brain trust aboard *Mighty Mary* made some questionable calls, and then Conner had passed them. Dellenbaugh may have technically made the right calls, but given the extreme conditions, he failed to protect the lead. *Stars & Stripes* won by 52 seconds. No one could believe this was happening. *Stars & Stripes* became the defender. Once again, Dennis, with the help of veteran tactician Tom Whidden and the never-say-die crew, rose like a phoenix from the ashes.

And now all hands had to prepare for The America's Cup, May 6-20, a best of nine races series. There was yet another surprise in store: Team Dennis Conner decided to replace *Stars & Stripes* with *Young America*, a move accomplished by the payment of a very substantial charter fee to PACT '95. The reasoning was that *Young America* had the best record, and if Team Dennis Conner didn't select the *fastest* of the American boats, he would be criticized. Others thought it would be difficult to fully acquaint the *Stars & Stripes*' crew, in such a short time, with an unfamiliar boat.

A very unhappy camper was *Stars & Stripes*' designer Dave Pedrick who went public with his disapproval. I tried to dissuade him from doing so. Understandably, he believed that "his" *Stars & Stripes* was entitled to face *NZL 32* after winning the defender trials.

As it turned out, it would not have mattered either way. *Black Magic* was longer, narrower, heavier and faster, and she lived up to her performance. As so often in the past (as would happen again in 2000), the Cup races were anticlimactic when compared to the desperately fought trials. *Black Magic*, in beating the defender in five straight races, averaged three-minute wins, just about the same margin as the New Zealanders had beaten the other challengers.

Peter Blake and his team had had a rigorous two new boat program, similar to the program Dennis Conner had first developed in his successful *Freedom* defense in 1980. The defending syndicates each had only one new boat. It is highly unlikely that any one-boat program will ever win over a well-managed two-boat effort. If anyone can pull it off I would bet on Dennis. He felt he could do it in Auckland in the year 2000, and might have, *if only…*

My America's Cup insider's experience doesn't always relate to the larger sailing issues. There were many unforgettable small moments. In 1994 the New York Yacht Club had a wonderful celebration in Newport commemorating its 150th anniversary. Among others, Bill Koch and Dennis showed up to race in IACC boats. Bill had invited the *Stars & Stripes* group to a crew party. At one point, Dennis made a disparaging remark about the *Mighty Mary* women. Designer Bruce Nelson's beautiful wife, a world class sailor and crew on *Mighty Mary*, overheard the comment and promptly poured her drink over DC. Visibly upset afterwards, she was afraid she would be fired which, of course, she wasn't.

While in Newport, Bill Koch asked if I would advise him as to what he should pay for a large framed Dennis Conner watercolor. In a weak moment, Bill had suggested a very large sum. As requested, I discussed this important financial transaction with DC. A generous payment was made on the theory that "bread cast upon the waters…" I have often wondered where Bill Koch has it displayed. Next to a Monet, perhaps?

The 1983 America's Cup ended the era of a yacht club running its own defense, an era that lasted for a period of 113 years (1870 – 1983). After that, budgets increased dramatically, with corporations, instead of individuals, becoming the prime source of funds. The Cup became an event open to the entire sporting world, rather than to the private world of yachting. Each succeeding campaign brought forth organizations to run the defense/challenge on behalf of the involved yacht clubs, which were anxious to insulate themselves from financial risk.

After the 1995 Cup, Terry Harper, executive director of U.S. Sailing, wrote: "…responsibility of a yacht club to run an America's Cup perhaps should be placed in the hands of a professional organization." And the commodore of the Royal New Zealand Yacht Squadron on January 25, 2000, released a memorandum titled "The Case for Reorganization of the America's Cup." In the new millennium, the evolution will proceed. The America's Cup will remain the oldest sporting trophy in continuous competition.

I must add that although San Diego Yacht Club had been subjected to heavy criticism during its nine-year Cup custodianship, I think they deserve "The Grand Gesture" for the constructive changes made during this period.

CHAPTER 8

DENNIS

uch has been covered about Dennis Conner in the chapters relating to individual campaigns. But he continues to be such an integral part of this event, as his nickname "Mr. America's Cup" attests, it is impossible not to add further recollections about this man who has successfully defended the America's Cup four times. The challenge he's leading for the New York Yacht Club in 2003 will be his ninth venture into this fray.

Before the 1974 defense of the America's Cup, my only knowledge of Dennis Conner had come from reading about his various exploits racing in the Southern Ocean Racing Circuit (SORC), as well as racing Star boats. It was not until the *Mariner* syndicate was established by former commodore of the New York Yacht Club George Hinman for the 1974 defense of the America's Cup that I ran across his name again. Dennis had been selected to be tactician for Ted Turner and my son Richard was the navigator for this effort. During the construction of *Mariner* and early practices, many of the crew lived with us, however, neither Dennis nor Ted Turner was introduced to me during this phase. Both my wife Eleanor and I decided it would be best if we steered clear of the *Mariner* program, to avoid any parental interference.

Late in the summer of 1974, we sailed to Newport to watch the Cup boats from a respectable distance. One day as we were sailing along enjoying the sight of these 12-meters on Rhode Island Sound, *Mariner* purposefully approached us. Dennis, at the helm, called across the water asking what I thought the wind would do.

I was taken aback, and wondered why, with all the brains on board, he would want my opinion. But I answered, "Looks like it will come in from the southwest"

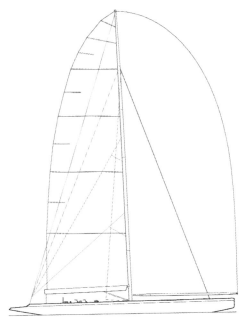

2000

STARS & STRIPES SYNDICATE

CHAIRMAN / MANAGER
Dennis Conner

SKIPPER
Ken Read

OPERATIONS MANAGER
Bill Trenkle

DESIGNER
Reichel-Pugh

BUILDER
New England Boat Works

(pretty safe; it usually did). That was the extent of my first and only conversation with him until 1979. Later, I learned that Dennis never hesitated to ask for a second or third opinion no matter how much information he had on hand, and he usually had quite a bit.

In 1976, I became manager of the *Enterprise* syndicate. One of our first challenges was to select a skipper. Our newly formed management committee of Fritz Jewett, Admiral Kinney and myself, with some outside input, developed a list of the 20 leading sailors of the day, including Ted Turner and Dennis Conner. After frank discussions, we selected Lowell North whose credentials were outstanding. Our decision to bypass Turner and Conner was based on concerns relating to personality issues. If we had known then Dennis' strengths – leadership, organization, respect for a budget and exemplary work ethic – as we later came to know them, I for one would have pushed hard for his selection. But everyone liked Lowell and respected his sailing record. What we didn't know was the extent of his ability to *lead* a contender to a successful defense of the America's Cup.

The time came in 1977 when Lowell was asked to step down as skipper of *Enterprise* under heavy pressure from our major backers and the America's Cup Committee. I contacted Dennis, who was in Europe for the World Star Boat Championship, and asked if he would consider taking over. He understandably turned down our invitation, no surprise to me. He wasn't interested in coming in at the last moment, nor did he want to withdraw from the Star competition. As it happened, he won this classic event with five firsts, a record that still stands. Malin Burnham, *Enterprise*'s upwind helmsman, took over as skipper and did his best, but the die had already been cast.

In spite of our loss to *Courageous* in 1977, our organization was intact and ready for another try in 1980. At a reception, held at Salve Regina College in Newport, I finally met Dennis face to face. He was physically imposing and quite relaxed. I bluntly asked if he would like to skipper a new defender in the next Cup defense. He said he would consider it. I had the feeling that he had anticipated my question. It turned out that Dennis was very good at anticipating questions.

This meeting led to an introduction to the most important member-team of our syndicate – George F. Jewett, Jr. (Fritz), and his wife Lucy. We all met at the Jewett's summer home in Wood's Hole. Their home was quietly impressive and Dennis was anxious to make a proper impression. At lunch, iced tea was served. Dennis, with much grace, began spooning salt from a small glass dish to his tea. Lucy, with a glint in her eye, asked Dennis if he usually used salt instead of sugar. Of course the answer was no, and this served to "break the ice." We all had a good laugh, including Dennis. After lunch we sat down for a serious talk.

In a previous chapter I commented on the three issues Dennis raised: treatment of his family; a no-cut contract as skipper (other than for reasons of health); and a two-boat campaign. This last request scared me but not the Jewetts. The proposal was approved.

There never were any written agreements. Our relationship was based on full respect for each other. The Jewetts and I were strictly volunteers as was Dennis. He did not expect, ask for, or receive any compensation for the 1980 *Freedom* campaign or the following defense in 1983. We did cover his direct expenses, such as infrequent trips between San Diego and Newport. Often he was accused of being paid. Let me be clear: he was not compensated, directly or indirectly. The campaigns of 1977, 1980, and 1983 were truly Corinthian programs.

We were off to a good start in 1980, with confidence and trust in each other. In our six campaigns together the Jewetts, Dennis, and I never had a dispute. In the 1987 and subsequent campaigns of *Stars & Stripes*, the Jewetts and I continued our support and involvement though not in key management roles. Malin Burnham led the 1987, 1988, and 1992 campaigns.

Let's go back to 1974. Ted Turner was skipper and Dennis Conner tactician. On her first trial run out of Mamaroneck in a light southwester, the Britton Chance-designed, Bob Derektor-built Mariner was sailing to windward. From on board my *Lady Del*, I observed *Mariner*'s movements along with my wife and Andy MacGowan, who was the key instigator of our 1977 campaign and a crew member of *Intrepid*'s (1974) and *Enterprise*'s (1977) efforts. Hardly five minutes had passed when Eleanor observed, "She is slow, dragging a body." I snapped back, "What do you know about it? Brit Chance knows what he's doing....she's been tank tested, and has the latest underbody."

What a disaster this design turned out to be! This was not the only time Eleanor spotted a weakness before I did. She was exceptionally good at sizing up people, and boats – for better or for worse.

In desperation, *Mariner* was returned to the Mamaroneck yard, where Bob Derecktor himself, wielding a chainsaw, sawed off the stern with no hesitation. A conventional stern was designed and installed. Not only did *Mariner* miss important practice and trial racing, but she still proved to be slow.

Later in that summer, Dennis took over as skipper of *Mariner*. Except for the starts, *Mariner* was out of it. The supposedly breakthrough design just didn't work. It shook confidence in the small scale models used in developing most of the 12-meter yachts. This led to the larger one-third scale model adopted in the *Enterprise* campaign of 1977.

Any change of skipper is dramatic and traumatic. Naturally the emotional Ted Turner was frustrated and upset. The crew was upset. The amazing Turner convinced his crew to stick together and do their best for Dennis. They did, but *Mariner* just didn't stand a chance.

Following *M*'s elimination, Dennis was invited to join the *Courageous* after guard as starting helmsman and tactician. The game of "musical chairs" was being played on *Courageous*. At one point Bob Bavier was the skipper with the veteran Jack Sutphen as tactician. Bob McCullough, syndicate head, who resurrected the 1977 *Courageous* campaign, was calling the shots. Ted Hood had shipped his *Robin* abroad, where he had intended to race her. The transport ship had a propeller problem, and had to be towed back. This freed up Ted, and opened the way for McCullough to replace Bavier with Hood. The veteran Jack Sutphen was Bavier's tactician. To improve the starts, Sutphen was replaced by Dennis. This was a hard blow for both Bavier and Sutphen, but they handled their removal in a sportsmanlike manner. Sutphen's attitude made an impression on Dennis who later invited him to join his future Cup campaigns.

Sailing on *Courageous* was to become the first of Dennis' four America's Cup victories. Gerry Driscoll was the capable skipper of the old *Intrepid*, which was in a dramatic death struggle with the new *Courageous*. Driscoll, understandably, was concerned about Dennis Conner's aggressive starting maneuvers. These starts were based on Dennis' confidence in his ability to judge time and distance. He developed this ability by *always* playing games with some of his after guard, making bets on when they would reach a specific buoy, then making as tight a turn as possible. This could be disconcerting when he used the same technique driving his car.

On the very last day of racing, *Courageous* eliminated *Intrepid*. Certainly, the

Courageous-Intrepid defense trials that summer were as close as any that have taken place.

Dennis didn't forget Jack Sutphen (who was then employed at Ratsey & Lapthorn, well known sailmakers, once suppliers to Admiral Nelson). After Dennis became associated with our *Freedom* campaign, he invited Jack to lunch, and asked him to consider working with him. Jack at first thought this was for a few months. Dennis said it was to be for the duration. This led Jean and Jack Sutphen to leave their beloved Larchmont for San Diego, where Jack continues to work closely with Dennis.

Dennis would often remember the strong points of crew members he had run across at one time or another, and was not to be dissuaded when he had decided upon a recruit. An example of his persistence was his first meeting in Florida with his future capable and often very humorous tactician, Tom Whidden. He invited Tom to join him in a syndicate effort. Tom wasn't ready to say yes. When Dennis learned that Tom was to fly north to his Essex home, Dennis was on the same plane, and ended up as Tom's house guest. Finally, Tom agreed (perhaps as a means to rid himself of his visitor). What a wonderful team they have been.

Dennis, admittedly a complex individual, has nonetheless attracted some outstanding people to work with him through the years. He does not hesitate to use people to help him and when his mind is preoccupied, he will ignore even his closest associates. But those working with him inevitably get caught up in the sheer excitement of a Conner-led competition; they recognize his capabilities and successes, even when he loses. They learn to roll with the negatives.

Dennis was a frequent guest in our Sands Point, New York, home. We found him to be relaxed and not without a sense of humor. After an overnight flight from San Diego, he arrived at our house with his clothes quite wrinkled. He was to be guest speaker at a gathering of our local yacht clubs. As always, he had a solution. He hung his jacket and pants in the guest bathroom, opened three hot water faucets, and closed the door. After some time had passed, Eleanor heard the water running. When she opened the door, solid steam greeted her. We turned off the water, and opened the window. The jacket and pants were fine, but the steam had caused the wallpaper to peel off the wall.

Over the years, Dennis has called me to discuss this problem, or that plan, and he always *has* a plan. Each time we'd talk I could be sure he had already thought the main points through. I would jot down these thoughts, usually agreeing with him as he went along. This is still my modus operandi. Later, after I have gone over each item and made my notes, I get back to him. He listens, but rarely, if ever, acknowledges whether or not he agrees with my responses. Even so, I know he hears them and takes them seriously. In most instances, he accepts my suggestions.

In my experience, Dennis never hesitated to ask a crew, friend, or stranger what he thought about a particular issue. He really wanted the input to match it against his own ideas. Rather than give a direct crew order, he often would ask if an adjustment should be made to a particular piece of equipment. He encouraged his crews to act on their own initiative.

Directly criticizing a person, much less firing anyone, were things Dennis did not like to do. Someone else would have to lower the axe. Guess who. These instances, often quite sticky, were always true tests of my empathy and tact.

Dennis was not formally educated in financial matters, but he is naturally respectful of budgets and organization. If our budget was running tight, Dennis understood that he had to hold back, and he did. If there was something he need-ed for the campaign and we didn't have the funds, he would go out and raise the money himself.

As syndicate manager responsible to the Maritime College Foundation for the budget, I found Dennis easy to work with. During the three campaigns, under the aegis of the Maritime College Foundation, we never were in the red, nor did the Foundation ever have to borrow money. One of the key reasons was Dennis' understanding of "a balanced budget," a concept he adhered to in his personal life as well. He ran his drapery business on a conservative, hands-on basis. His personal affairs were kept private, and we all respected that. I never bought his claim that he was a "poor country boy." He is self-made and very smart.

During the *Freedom* 1980, and *Liberty* 1983 campaigns, he was openly accused of being a professional. Ted Turner was quite vocal about this. Dennis certainly did approach his sailing projects in a professional manner. Ted Hood and Lowell North, as sailmakers, could be considered "professionals," in that they earned their living from sailing-related businesses. Of course, they were not paid to serve as skippers. Dennis was a drapery salesman and he, too, was not paid for being skipper. In fact, the 1980 and 1983 campaigns adversely affected his drapery busi-ness, taking him away from that aspect of his life.

Sailing was definitely Dennis' first priority, family and business included. Even though such priorities would not be mine, such focus and concentration did enable him to become the sailing legend he is. For Turner, sailing at one time also seemed to have come first, or maybe it was winning the America's Cup, or possi-bly thumbing his nose at what he considered the yachting establishment.

When in San Diego, Dennis would get me up around 6 AM, and drive me to his office and drapery plant where I would accompany him on his daily morning business routine. He checked the mail, and would go from one factory station to another, always asking about problems and listening closely to those described. He would check the work orders, and then call customers directly to be sure they were getting proper service. On his regular morning schedule, after his visit to his factory and office, shortly after 0900, he would be at the San Diego Yacht Club.

Dennis also showed me his company's books, which were simple but set up to give an instant picture of where he stood. He was proud that he carried no inventory of his own; he was running the business so efficiently that he only needed to stock some Kirsch curtain rods. In his livelihood he was a complete professional. And he sure knew all aspects of his operation. On one of his visits to our home, our draperies had just come back from the cleaners. Without any hesitation, he hung them for us in a matter of minutes.

n Newport, just before the 1980 Cup races began, the tail end of a hurricane passed by. We had hauled *Freedom* for safety. In those days our insurance carrier reimbursed us for any such preventive expense. The next day, with winds over 30 knots (and about 40 over the deck), Dennis took *Freedom* out. I was on board along with a TV sports broadcaster. As we lurched through heavy seas, the latter asked DC what was he thinking about in a taped interview. Dennis answered "I'm wondering whether we will lose our f---ing mast." I have a video of this conversation with Dennis' uncharacteristic response. He rarely cursed.

During one of Dennis' visits to our home, George Hinman and Harman Hawkins, both NYYC conservatives, joined us. I had casually mentioned that Dennis rarely, if ever, cursed. This in itself was quite unusual for the stressed-out position of skipper, or was before there were the ever-present ears of onboard microphones. Later that evening we sat around the TV to view the tape. Everyone got a laugh when I showed the video interview on board *Freedom*. I am not sure Dennis was particularly amused.

While Dennis was often tense and distracted ashore, the moment he set foot on board a boat his personality changed. In this element, he would be calm and relaxed. If guests were on board he would joke with them. Often he could sense that something was not right. For instance, he could hear/feel bad vibrations of the rigging, and have the anomaly adjusted before it turned into a full-blown problem.

Giving direct orders was not something Dennis felt comfortable with, so he didn't do that very often. His crew would know his intention from a question he might ask. For instance, he might ask JW (Jon Wright), a many-time veteran of Cup campaigns, what he thought of the outhaul, rather than order the outhaul to be eased.

Dennis perceives his role and priorities differently today. Bear in mind that my personal observations primarily relate to the campaigns in which I was most closely associated with him, 1980-1983-1987, and, to a somewhat lesser degree, 1988-1992-1995. In the more recent years, an older Dennis Conner has taken on other roles, culminating in his making a substantial financial success from America's Cup activities, Dennis Conner Sports, and the Whitbread Round-the-World program. In addition, he has remarried and become a successful artist.

In the more recent campaigns he was smart enough to turn over the helm to Paul Cayard (1995) and Ken Read (2000). This freed him up to manage the campaigns and to raise money.

For many years Dennis participated in the Congressional Cup in Long Beach, California, still a prestigious big boat match race series, where he did extremely well. But once he became deeply immersed in the America's Cup, he has generally avoided other match racing events.

Today he continues to distinguish himself in the very competitive Etchell-22 class, and maintains a fleet of small boats which he races in San Diego. While visiting me in the dead of one winter, he asked about our local frostbite racing. He said he would like to try it. It was no problem to borrow an Interclub dinghy for him. This is a single-sail, Sparkman & Stephens design. Dennis is no lightweight, but in the 11' 6" dinghy he sailed off in the icy waters of Manhasset Bay with a young crew. He lost the first race, his "learning experience," then simply began to win.

Dennis commissioned Ken Gardiner, a model expert, to build a full set of America's Cup challengers and defenders for him, similar in scale to those on private display at the New York Yacht Club. The collection was completed for a substantial sum. He frequently loaned out these beautiful models. I think his desire to have such a collection relates to his frustrated relationship with the New York Yacht Club. He recently told me he has sold the collection. You can bet he didn't lose any money on the sale.

As mentioned, when driving a car or boat of any kind, Dennis would usually come as close as possible to a curb or buoy to improve his time and distance judgment. Dollar bets with Halsey Herreshoff, John Marshall, Tom Whidden (or virtually anyone handy), as to how long it would take to reach a mark or object, or how far away it might be, sharpened his senses. He did not lose very often. At his home, he had sophisticated pinball machines, with a cupful of quarters at hand. At every opportunity, he would challenge anyone available to play against him. Here was another exercise to sharpen his skills. And another mode of expression for a serious competitor.

In 1983 during a sail on *Magic* in very heavy seas off Brenton Reef, Dennis was driving the boat hard upwind. At one point, the bow went under as did the entire foredeck. Adam Ostenfeld was at the pointy end. You couldn't see him below the knees. I have the photos to prove it. The crew was yelling "Dive, dive," as *Magic* did a creditable imitation of a submarine. Privately, I was hoping she would keep going down (*Magic* was not performing as well as hoped; we could have used the insurance money).

One foggy morning off Castle Hill (Newport), Dennis sailed *Freedom* past a lobster boat at a pretty fast clip causing it to roll. Angry lobstermen yelled at Dennis. The next morning, Dennis arose early, found the lobstermen as he was leaving the dock, and asked if he could ride along. He did, and all was forgiven. Dennis has a good appreciation of the working man.

From some of the stories about *Freedom* and *Magic*, one might think Dennis irresponsible. This was far from the case. As I have recounted in the chapter about the catamaran-versus-*NZ 1* race in 1988, Dennis capsized in order to test the limits of a multi-hull. As usual, he had winning on his mind. By incorporating experienced catamaran sailors for this campaign, as well as the best catamaran designers and builders, and also by pushing the envelope of possibility sailing the boats, he was simply, once again, doing what was necessary to win.

When Dennis was preparing for his challenge to "Bring Back The Cup" in 1987, he was roundly criticized by the press, and others, for not bringing his boats to Fremantle to practice in the waters where the Cup races were to be held. Again, I have dealt with this in the appropriate chapter. It simply serves to point out that Dennis was often misinterpreted by the press. He rarely made the effort to change public perception, while he made sure the people who mattered in his universe knew what he was doing. In the 1987 incident, the lesson of the day became obvious: If *Stars & Stripes* had been in Australia, they would have been sailing in mostly light winds. But in Hawaii, the crew was able to do that *and* practice in heavier weather. Remember, the challenge to the designers was to design a boat that could survive the eliminations, conducted in mostly light weather, and then be able to win the Cup in heavier weather. Here Dennis had the best of both worlds, plus a far less expensive operation than he would have had in Australia. They also were able to operate with little interference and few distractions. Good thinking, Dennis.

Chairman Burnham had asked me to go to Fremantle in August of 1986 to help establish the *S & S* organization on the defender's turf. This I regretfully was unable to do. I promised that Eleanor and I would arrive early in December and stay to the very end. It was no surprise to find that Dennis and his team had set up a first class operation in their new compound long before we arrived. Much of the credit goes to his right hand man Bill Trenkle, a Maritime College graduate.

Eleanor and I spent several days in Sydney before proceeding to Fremantle. The reader will recall the episode with the Sydney taxi driver regarding Dennis' accusation that the Kiwis had cheated by using fibreglass. The irate man considered it an insult to all New Zealanders.

Dennis often drew criticism when he fixed on ideas like this one, ideas planted without substantiation and then publicly repeated. And he bore the brunt of the criticism. These types of statements would normally originate after a long, hard day of racing, sometimes when he was confronted at a press conference. Such outbursts did keep Dennis' name in the headlines and add spice to the contest, but they didn't help his public image.

Arriving in Fremantle, Roberta Burnham, Judy Conner and Dot Chesebrough met us. A very comfortable townhouse was to be our home. Next to us were the Burnhams, Whiddens and the Conners. The first night, Malin and DC came over. Dennis, exhausted, after a very full day, stretched out on the floor. They asked if I would coordinate a drive to raise more funds. I had been receiving periodic financial reports and, of course, had helped in the fund raising.

This operation was not as simple as it was when we were in Newport. A budget triple the size of the previous campaign and headquarters some 8,000 miles away from home were going to complicate matters.

I had little confidence in the updated financials. Malin told me that they were behind several million dollars. I suggested that they bring the books to Fremantle where I could work with the staff to check them out. After we had a chance to do that, we could then take steps to close the gap.

Sandy Purdon, Sail America's Executive Administrator, brought the financials from San Diego to Fremantle for review. After several days, we came to the conclusion that the deficit was substantially higher. Malin and Dennis met in our condo. Malin relaxed in a chair. In fact, Malin is always relaxed. I passed out legal pads. From my notes, I would call out names of those past supporters who had not responded, as well as others we might approach. We would write down the names of those each of us would follow up. Since most all the contacts were in the U.S., we found ourselves phoning at 11 p.m., or later each evening. Dennis, Malin and I would do our full share and, in the morning, I would pick up the reports. It paid off, as we took a large bite out of the deficit. The first few calls brought in over $200,000. As *Stars & Stripes* went on her winning way, it became easier. I volunteered to call upon the well-known American financier, Bill Simon, on his large S&S designed sailing yacht, *Freedom*, moored in Fremantle. We had an interesting conversation during lunch, but no brass ring.

When it appeared that Dennis would become the challenger, Arthur Santry, the straight-laced commodore of the New York Yacht Club, approached me. He was concerned about Dennis' drinking, suggesting that if it continued, it would embarrass the Cup and the New York Yacht Club. I assured him that this would never be the case. However, I decided to talk to Dennis at the proper moment. That opportunity arrived when Dennis suggested we take a drive so he could show me around town.

I opened the Santry issue by saying to Dennis that he was his own person and that we all understood the great pressure he was under from the press, Blackaller, New Zealand, et cetera. I said that I have known many drinkers, some funny, some pleasant. But I mentioned that when DC has a drink he becomes moody and can say things that he shouldn't, sometimes insulting those nearby. With the heaviest competition ahead, and even greater pressure, I suggested that he might want to be extra careful.

Dennis listened but didn't respond. Until the final victory, there were no further problems on that score. Perhaps Commodore Santry should have asked what brand of liquor he was drinking. When Abe Lincoln was advised of General Ulysses S. Grant's intemperance, he said he would like to send the same brand of liquor to his other generals. Ted Turner wasn't adverse to a drink or two, as was occasionally apparent during his successful 1977 Cup defense.

Over the years of our association, Dennis did have difficulties with the press. Even on land, he was focused on sailing, often tired and harassed. But when a reporter was invited on the Cup boat during a practice or on a sail to or from our base, Dennis always enjoyed the conversation that would follow, as did the reporter. In Fremantle, the press often reported inaccuracies, which strained the relationship even more. It was quite upsetting to all of us as that campaign approached its climax.

Back in 1980, I had been having a difficult time keeping feathers unruffled, as Dennis shied away from the reporters who were milling around our compound gate each day. I asked Joanne Fishman, a sportswriter for the *New York Times*, to help me. She wrote an outline of what Dennis should do to make life easier for him and the press. We set up a special time for the press to be at the gate. I gave Dennis Joanne's suggestions. Over the years, Dennis has become much more at ease with the media, although he never really enjoyed the attention from the press, particularly when under pressure.

After winning back the Cup from Australia, Dennis' schedule became even heavier. Business propositions, invitations to speak, requests to sign books and posters came in by the droves. I had been asked by the president of Green Mountain College, in Poultney, Vermont, if Dennis would be the keynote speaker at their 153rd graduation ceremony. With some hesitation, because of the heavy demands on Dennis, I asked him if he would consider doing this, for which he was to receive an honorary degree. He asked my connection. I told him I was a trustee for over 20 years, and that my daughter Cathy had graduated from there. He quickly agreed.

The night of his arrival at the college, after dinner, he asked if I would assist him while he signed a large number of Mystic Seaport Cup posters. Until the wee hours of the morning he signed, while proudly telling me in detail the state of his finances and his future plans.

I have said that Dennis always described himself as a "poor country boy." I never questioned him about it, but I didn't believe it for a minute. While that tag may have applied to his early days when he was hanging around the San Diego Yacht Club docks, he no doubt found some advantage in continually playing up his role as underdog. He did it again in 2000 in New Zealand. But back to Green Mountain College:

The next morning, after almost an all night poster signing session, we were given our robes and mortar boards. Dennis asked me on which side to hang the tassel. "How would I know?" I said. " I never graduated from college either."

Dennis gave a superb speech about dedication and commitment, relating a Cup campaign to a college experience. When President Pollock bestowed the degree on Dennis, he referred to him as the "The Fremantle Doctor," a reference to the heavy sea breeze which had paid an afternoon call each day during the 1987 Cup races. I was quite proud of Dennis that day. He was very warmly received.

After the ceremony, walking in the procession Dennis broke ranks and approached me with a gleam in his eye. He asked if I would like to see his notes, and showed me the palms of his hand. They were clean.

This took me back to the summer of 1980. When we set up our crew house in Newport, we established a routine. Each evening after supper (for about forty of us), there would be various announcements relating to crew schedule, public appearances, birthdays, guests. In 1977, Lowell North, who was somewhat shy, had left the announcements to me. When Dennis came aboard, he agreed to do this evening chore. Early on, he would ask me what items to cover and make ink notes on the palms of his hands. Now, seven years later, he was proving to me that he no longer needed any notes. Indeed he didn't.

In 1980, one of our crew was Arnie Schmeling (referred to as the "killer cop") from Long Beach, California. He was related to the famous German boxer, Max. Arnie would effectively put us through our exercise drills each morning beginning at 0600 on the Seaview Terrace lawn (this crew workout also included the Jewetts,

Jack Sutphen, and me). After stretching, we would jog around Newport. Arnie would lead the team, I would bring up the rear with Dennis. At a point, Dennis would peel off onto a side street with me alongside taking a little short cut. Once Arnie got wise he joined us in the rear, putting a stop to our little diversion. (In 1995, Arne was hired by Bill Koch to guard his Botero statues while in San Diego, and was kind enough one day to take us on a "museum" tour.)

One morning, Jack Sutphen was missing from the exercise routine. We shouted up to his window from which a white bedsheet eventually flapped in the breeze. Jack had surrendered.

In 1987, with everyone still in a daze from our Australian victory, and trying to get back to a normal schedule, along came the surprise New Zealand challenge. Without a chance to catch his breath Dennis was asked to accept the responsibility of skippering a defender. He took heavy abuse for the selection of a catamaran as the defender against the monster monohull *NZ 1*. Although he felt strongly that the challenge had been a sneak attack, it was not his decision to use a catamaran. That decision belonged to the San Diego Yacht Club. As expected, Dennis went all out to defend the Cup in 1988. Once again John Marshall took a leading role in organizing and leading the design team.

The 1992 defense in the spectacular new IACC leading-edge boats was complicated, time consuming, and expensive. Dennis raised a major share of corporate funds, as he had done in 1987, hoping to have two new boats, without which a syndicate has little chance to win. (Dennis felt he could win, however, with one boat in the year 2000 – and while he did not win, he made a creditable showing, *very* creditable given his very modest budget).

The financial giants, such as Bill Koch (USA), and the late Raul Gardini (Italy), developed programs in 1992 that may never be exceeded in expense, in number of boats, or intensity of design effort. It was a difficult time to raise funds, in part because of the unpopular catamaran defense in 1988, and Dennis was primarily responsible for the fund raising. To build a second boat Dennis would have had to go into debt. Borrowing money is against his nature. On a visit to San Diego, I met with Dennis. We discussed the alternatives. I said to Dennis that, either way, he couldn't lose. With one boat and crew he would be the underdog against the massive Koch machine. Dennis would not be daunted by staggering odds. His reputation would not suffer, and he would contribute to the success of the defense without going into debt. I'm sure he had figured all this out for himself. Certainly, Dennis wanted to win, but he was well aware of the facts of life. Besides, he would continue his involvement with the America's Cup since this was a prime source of income to him. Stimulated by the worldwide television coverage and onboard cameras used during the 1987 Australian defense, commercialism had taken hold in a big way, and the America's Cup competition had gone the way of golf, tennis, football, and other major sports. This was no longer the Corinthian sport of bygone days (1983 and earlier).

I was told by several veteran sportswriters that no sport celebrity gave to his corporate sponsors as much attention and care as Dennis did. I can attest to this. Not only did Dennis give talks to staffs of various corporate sponsors, he was continuously pushed into late dinners with corporate executives and special customers. He had to be available even on racing days. Dennis stretched himself thin, perhaps too thin, usually starting his day around 5:00 a.m. having had as much sleep as Winston Churchill during World War II. As a further comparison, I must note that Churchill's well-known imbibing did not interfere in the least with his leadership responsibilities.

Dennis' extremely heavy schedule included fund raising, responsibility for developing a viable team, meeting press demands, keeping up with his business interests, those dinner meetings with sponsors and their customers, as well as giving attention to syndicate supporters. Obviously, his family life, and his business suffered. The corporate sponsors received more than their money's worth.

During a visit to our home in the early '90's, Dennis showed us some sailing sketches he had made on airline stationery. In his "spare" moments, he began to create some interesting America's Cup racing scenes. Dennis has since been successful in marketing his artwork. During the round robin racing early in 2000 in New Zealand, Dennis sent Eleanor and me one of his own numbered Cup scenes, autographed by his crew with a special inscription from him.

By the 1995 defense, Dennis had remarried, and his mind was not as fully involved in the team's daily operations. There was more delegation of responsibilities, less early morning participation down at the compound. He invited the charismatic Paul Cayard to skipper *Stars & Stripes*. It worked out smoothly, as there was a strong mutual respect between these long time sailing rivals.

This made me think back to my suggestion to the New York Yacht Club, after losing the Cup in 1983, that John Kolius understudy Dennis with the idea that he could eventually wind up driving a Dennis Conner Cup boat. In spite of Cayard's aggressive attitudes over the years when competing against Dennis, the association was a good one. Dennis pretty much allowed Paul to run the boat, recognizing that something had to give, with his new domestic life on top of his responsibilities for organizing and funding a campaign. Paul's experience working with Dennis in 1995, I'm sure, gave him the courage to lead his St. Francis Yacht Club challenge for the 30th America's Cup (year 2000).

Dennis was not too happy with the design of his new 1995 IACC boat. Some of the experiments went awry, like when the twin keel foils drove her sideways, or when she almost sank. As always, his crew was outstanding. The work load thrust upon the ground support team led by another Conner stalwart, Mick Harvey, was as heavy as I ever witnessed. Through all of the near disasters Dennis would not rave or rant. It was just another challenge to be met. He would let off steam on occasion, but it would never be on board. Dennis is tough and will rise to the occasion. He has always had crew loyalty. The crew respects his work ethic as well as his on-the-water performance. We all liked to be with a winner. Even when Dennis didn't win, we all stood proud.

Gary Jobson wrote in *Yachting* Magazine (March 1977), "I had the good fortune of racing with many of the world's best sailors, including Ted Turner, Buddy Melges, the late Tom Blackaller, and Dennis Conner. Conner is the quietest skipper I have sailed with. The more chaotic the situation, the more control and focus he displays."

Dennis was on the verge of elimination more than once. Through Conner "luck" and the mistakes of others, he seemed to have nine lives. In 1995, John Marshall let Dennis breathe again, and DC took him to the cleaners. The defender was ultimately routed, but once again Dennis had made the headlines.

Win or lose, Dennis never lacked for willing sailors or workers. When he developed the two-crew team in 1980, there was a general opinion that it wouldn't work. The question was whether anyone could keep two crews happy over an extended period of time. Dennis' answer to that was his extremely careful selection of sailors, including cadets from the Maritime College hand-picked by that school's waterfront director, Dick Chesebrough. In my association with Dennis and through the various America's Cup campaigns, there never was a serious crew problem. Dennis was more interested in attitude than vast experience, leaning heavily on a core of experienced crew to help develop young, new blood. He was willing to accept women on the team. Outstanding was Dory Street, a cadet from Maritime, who later married another Maritime product, Scott Vogel, probably the best bow man who ever sailed with Dennis.

I never asked a team member why he would give so much of himself to being part of Team Dennis Conner. But perhaps it was for the same reasons Fritz Jewett, Jack Sutphen, Dick Chesebrough…and I…continued to work so closely with Dennis. For us it certainly had nothing to do with financial compensation. We were never paid. And until 1987, neither were our crews. Dennis engendered such continuing respect and appreciation because we respected his willingness to learn from his seniors; his intelligence; his work ethic; his concern for careful use of funds and assets entrusted to him; his on-the-water performance under all conditions; and his outstanding ability to train a crew who could react instantly to an onboard emergency without prodding from Dennis. And last, but certainly not least, Dennis is a winner.

As gathered from earlier chapters, DC has two personalities—one on land, one on sea. To get to his "star " status, he had to devote an inordinate amount of time to his pursuit of sailing, even at the expense of his private life.

Keeping a "second team" enthusiastic was the result to a great degree of Dennis' selection of Jack Sutphen as the skipper of his trial horse. Dennis did not hesitate to advance a crew member from Jack's boat to his own when that was appropriate. Jack created a real "esprit de corps." One was proud to be a "mushroom."

I would often sail with Jack against Dennis. I was astonished to find this perfect gentleman ashore was a tiger at the wheel, sometimes with a short fuse. The crew loved him in spite of his ire if the crew performed below his high standard. Sailing with Jack was a far cry from sailing with Dennis, who was always calm and quiet.

Once sailing with Dennis, I did a sloppy job on the running backstay. Dennis stared coldly at me. I said, "How come when I sail with Jack I am always perfect?" This became a standard joke – at my expense.

During the years I was associated with Dennis, he received lucrative offers to join competing groups or lead foreign syndicates. All of which he turned down. He had a strong aversion to sailing for any but an American effort. He considered Rod Davis and others "Benedict Arnolds." During one of the San Diego defenses he was offered a seven figure deal to transfer to another American syndicate. He said he would consider the offer only if he could bring his own crew. When this condition was rejected, the deal was off.

Perhaps because of his difficult childhood, Dennis had a deep respect for established institutions. He never hesitated to remind people his father was a fisherman. As a boy he would spend time at the San Diego Yacht Club (his family were not members). He would help clean boats, ask questions of local sailing heroes like Malin Burnham and Lowell North, work in a sail loft, crew for some of the members. He was befriended by Ash Bown and Alan Rafee who became important influences in his life. Maybe his humble beginnings account for Dennis' feeling that he is an outsider. My sense is that he wanted to become part of the "establishment." He wanted to be accepted. In many ways he has achieved this end, but not completely. (For more on Dennis' early days, read his book, *No Excuse to Lose*.)

nd from a local boy dock rat, yearning to be part of this other life, Dennis rose to become commodore of the impressive San Diego Yacht Club. He respected the New York Yacht Club as the most prestigious in the world, even as he was confounded by what he could only perceive as an East Cost establishment. He was indeed honored to defend the Cup for them. Dennis was most respectful of Past Commodore George Hinman, never calling him the familiar "George" but always "Commodore." During the days of *Freedom*, when Dennis visited me in Sands Point, he would make it a point to lunch with the commodore, and show him the blueprints of our Cup boats.

When Commodore Hinman was suffering from a fatal illness, of which all of us were aware, we invited him to visit our crew house for several days. Dennis took him sailing on *Freedom*, and gave him the helm. This was to be Hinman's last sail on an America's Cup boat.

Though Dennis respected many members of the New York Yacht Club as individuals, his relationship with the Club, as an entity, has not been a close one. He helped defend the Cup for them in 1974, and he defended successfully in 1980. He was (we were) the first to lose the Cup in 1983, but only after a close and valiant battle. Even though we who have been closely associated with him know Dennis to be a complex individual, the New York Yacht Club did not treat him with the respect he deserved when the Cup was lost to Australia. This, however, couldn't erase his desire or willingness to represent this austere institution.

After the loss of the Cup to Australia, at a formal reception in honor of Betsy Jewett's wedding, Dennis cornered me in the coat checkroom. He asked me to look over a short, concise plan as to how he would win the Cup back. Hardly the time or place, but I glanced through it. I asked how big a budget did he plan. He mentioned $15 million. I told him I was happy <u>not</u> to be the manager. That was three times our 1983 budget. I offered the comment that I knew he could do it and said I would help.

Following the loss of the Cup in 1983, the New York Yacht Club was considering various alternatives. One of the leading groups included John Kolius, as skipper, with substantial financial backing of his Texas friends. As he had told me, Dennis was hoping to get the chance to "Bring Back The Cup" to the Club for which he had lost it.

As recounted elsewhere, the night Dennis was to be inducted as Commodore of the San Diego Yacht Club happened to be the night he was "ordered" to New York to discuss a possible role in the NYYC's challenge. When he requested a more convenient time, it was denied.

This dogmatic approach scared Dennis. He made the decision, with the support of Malin Burnham and Fritz Jewett, to challenge on behalf of the SDYC instead. That weekend, there were a flurry of phone calls among the New York Yacht Club leadership, Fritz Jewett, and myself. The NYYC was advised that an announcement would be issued on Wednesday, that the SDYC would issue a challenge with Dennis as the skipper. This was a courtesy to permit them to make a simultaneous release. For some reason, the NYYC chose not to issue a press release at that time. Then they criticized San Diego for "jumping the gun," which, given the sequence of events, the San Diego Yacht Club had not done.

Prior to the loss to Australia, for many reasons not related to the America's Cup, I planned to retire from active America's Cup syndicate management. I was 70, Eleanor and I had become grandparents, and I wanted to return to sailing. To ensure that I wouldn't change my mind, I asked my friend Harold Oldak to help organize a group to have a fast cruising sailboat designed and built. I collaborated in the redesign of the Brewer 42. Thus, the Brewer 12.8 came into existence and I would get boat #10, to be delivered after the Cup campaign was over.

In December, 1983, without consulting anyone I met with Robert Stone, past commodore of NYYC, and the greatly respected and dynamic *unofficial* leader of the club. My recommendation was that the NYYC should invite Dennis to lead the challenge to regain the Cup (this too, I have dealt with on other pages in this memoir). I believed that I could get Dennis to agree that, if successful, he would turn over the helm to John Kolius for the following defense. For Kolius it would be a great opportunity to learn from the master. Commodore Stone's reaction was favorable. After several days, he advised me that Kolius wanted to be the skipper of the Club's challenger. The rest is history.

I waited ten or more years to tell Dennis of this proposal, which came as a surprise to him. When Dennis invited Paul Cayard to skipper his *Stars & Stripes* in 1995, and then Ken Read in 2000, I had to smile.

And in the year 2000 we were faced with the awesome challenge of wresting the Cup from the New Zealanders. There were a record number of challengers. New York had a well-prepared, heavily financed, and talented group. They had two new boats, designed by Bruce Farr, and had sailed in New Zealand more than most of the challengers. (It is interesting to note that Bruce Farr, an otherwise remarkably successful yacht designer, has not produced one America's Cup winner.)

John Marshall was the leader for the New York Yacht Club in the 2000 campaign, and one of the most experienced and brightest people on the America's Cup scene. Without his leadership in the design area, Dennis and Malin Burnham probably would not have brought back the Cup in 1987. However, John's only America's Cup successes (1980-1987-1988) were when he teamed up with Dennis.

Dennis would have liked to have been part of the NYYC team for the 2000 challenge. Early on several involved members of the NYYC had asked me what I thought would be the best way to organize a successful challenge. I knew how Dennis felt. He was prepared to shake hands with John Marshall, and raise a substantial fund toward their campaign. His prime interest was to handle the sailing phase, probably in a way similar to 1995, when he had turned over the helm to Paul Cayard. He was not interested in the overall responsibility. Having been closely involved with the past successes of Dennis and John Marshall as a team, I believed that would be the way to go. After considerable "on and off" discussions between Dennis, interested NYYC members, and myself, the matter was dropped.

Dennis ended up going to New Zealand with a one-new-boat effort, a good crew, and minimum on-the-water practice. Although I didn't believe that any one-boat effort would win, I had every confidence that Team Dennis Conner would add to the contest, the excitement, and interest, as they tried, once again, to eliminate the New York Yacht Club. Although a 20-year member of the New York Yacht Club, Dennis was still an "outsider."

The Cup races in the early part of 2000 found us for the first time since 1976 on the sidelines, with no regrets, but with many happy memories. Although Eleanor and I received several tempting invitations to visit New Zealand, including one from Dennis, family illness dictated otherwise. We did, of course, continue to follow the New Zealand defense closely, and with great interest, from our home, half the world away.

On December 13, 1999, at the time of *Young America*'s elimination, Dennis called me at 4:00 a.m. from New Zealand, asking me to approach the NYYC with a typical Dennis Conner imaginative idea. Dennis had great faith in the capability of *Stars & Stripes* to become the challenger. How could his club cross burgees with the NYYC and continue to keep the latter's hopes alive in the America's Cup of 2000?

If they jointly won it, he would consider bringing the event back to Newport. After a feverish eight hours, it was concluded that there was no legal or practical way this could be done.

As always, there are surprises. The most recent was the announcement by the New York Yacht Club and Dennis Conner that they have in fact joined hands to challenge for the Cup in 2003. Here at last, after an eighteen-year separation, Dennis has his wish to be representing the yacht club on 44th Street in New York. I am proud to have played a small part in bringing these forces together. And I fervently hope it will work out. Dennis' forte is fund raising and managing the campaign. He will respect the budget agreed upon, and have a first class crew, an all-American crew.

After three unsuccessful efforts, all of them learning experiences, some attained at considerable expense, I expect the latest New York Yacht Club challenge will put up a strong showing. There is no guarantee that we will win, but there is absolutely no question that Dennis and team will mount the good fight and walk away from the combat proudly. Interesting to consider that for the first time the New York Yacht Club will be the underdog facing "billionaire's row."

Dennis and I are in close touch as the plans unfold for the 2003 challenge. Dennis is working around the clock to raise funds, as only he can do, and is maintaining close contact with "his" eastern club.

Thinking about my relationship with Dennis, I enjoy remembering the cheers, the excitement, and the many wonderful experiences we shared. It gives me much satisfaction to know that he learned as much from me as I did from him. I eagerly await the starting gun, and the surprises which lie ahead.

CREDITS

Drawings courtesy of Reichel/Pugh on pages 2-3, 85
Drawings courtesy of Sparkman & Stephens on pages 11, 31
Drawings courtesy of Rolly Tasker on page 39
Drawing courtesy of Sail America on page 61
Drawings courtesy of David Pedrick on pages 49, 69, 77
Photos courtesy of Jack Sutphen on page 9; and photo insert page 2 bottom
Photos courtesy of Dan Nerney/DOT on pages 4, 7, 38, 44, 48, 54, 84, 90, 100;
and photo insert pages 5 bottom, 7 bottom
Photos courtesy of Dan Nerney page 76; and photo insert pages 5 top and middle, 8 top
Photos courtesy of the author on pages 3, 10, 16, 22, 30, 60, 64, 68, 72;
and photo insert pages 1, 2 right & left, 3, 4 (bottom is official White House photograph),
6, 7 top (official White House photograph), 8 left and bottom

Designed by Metze Publication Design
Set in Baskerville and Penumbra
Printed by Hamilton Printing